The People's Treasures

Collections in the National Library of Australia

Edited by John Thompson

National Library of Australia

© 1993 National Library of Australia

National Library of Australia Cataloguing-in-Publication entry
The People's treasures
    ISBN 0 642 10597 9.

    1. National Library of Australia. 2. National libraries—Collection
    development—Australian Capital Territory—Canberra. 3. Library
    resources—Australian Capital Territory—Canberra. I. Thompson,
    John (John Robert), 1947–   . II. National Library of Australia.
027.594

Publications Manager: Margaret Chalker
Publisher's editor: Carol Miller
Picture editor: Leora Kirwan
Designer: BPD Graphic Associates, Canberra
Printed by Inprint, Brisbane

FOREWORD

In August 1993 the Council and staff of the National Library of Australia join with the people of Australia in celebrating the 25th anniversary of the opening of the Library's handsome building on the shores of Lake Burley Griffin in Canberra. Since its doors were opened twenty-five years ago, the building has become an Australian landmark and one of the adornments of the national capital.

This book has been prepared as one of the means by which this notable anniversary is commemorated. Its purpose is to take readers inside the building and to provide some understanding of what the National Library of Australia represents to the people of this country: a great storehouse of information; a repository for the documentary heritage of our nation; and a resource for scholarship and for the exchange of ideas. The collections which have been built up over now nearly one hundred years are the asset of the Australian people. The treasures which the Library houses belong to all Australians. This book celebrates the collections which give the Library its heart and its purpose and which enrich and maintain a sense of national memory.

While celebrating the collections of the National Library of Australia, this book pays tribute both directly and indirectly to the many and various ways in which they have been developed and enriched. The support of government over the years has been of crucial importance but so too has been the generosity of many citizens of Australia and of distinguished donors and collectors who have lived overseas but who have shared a common interest in contributing to the strength of this notable Library. The book also acknowledges the work of successive generations of Library staff members who have pursued an ideal. The Library and its collections stand as a monument to this support.

Ninian Stephen
Chairman
National Library of Australia Council

ACKNOWLEDGEMENTS

The publication of this book owes special thanks to many people. But above all, it has been a team effort involving the willing collaboration of the seven other contributing authors who cheerfully met what must have seemed a daunting deadline. Also important was the enthusiastic cooperation of the curators and staff of the various collection areas represented in the book. Staff of the Library's publications section provided outstanding support, as did the photographic staff. Melissa Butler and Jan Sarah contributed invaluable administrative assistance. Special thanks are due to Hordern House Rare Books in Sydney and to Thomas Parkes in Canberra. The Library's Director-General, Warren Horton and its Assistant Director-General, Cultural and Educational Services, Ian Templeman provided the support and encouragement necessary to believe that the book could be produced at all.

CONTENTS

S T Gill. *Country NW of Tableland, Aug. 22,* painted from a sketch made during the Horrocks Expedition through the country north west of the Flinders Ranges, c.1846

INTRODUCTION
BOOKS AND MORE THAN BOOKS

John Thompson

Anniversaries of various kinds provide opportunities for assessing the achievements of the past and for contemplating the future. This book, conceived in the context of the celebrations to mark the twenty-five years since the National Library of Australia moved into its gracious building on the shores of Lake Burley Griffin in Canberra, is intended to open a window onto the Library's rich and diverse collection developed over a period now only a few years short of a full century. That more substantial anniversary will be celebrated in 2001, the year which marks the hundred years since the Commonwealth Parliamentary Library came into existence. It was within this library framework that an idealistic generation of librarians and politicians commenced the task of building the collections which today form the great heart of the National Library of Australia.

This book is not a history of the National Library. That task has not yet been undertaken though it is a potent story and one which must eventually be told. Nor is it a definitive account of the collections or even of all of the Library's significant materials. But through a sampling of works in a range of formats, it is intended to give some understanding of the evolution of the Library from its historical beginnings as a small, undefined and not particularly well-focused section within the Commonwealth Parliamentary Library to the complex collecting institution it has become in the late years of the twentieth century.

The title for this book derives from a recent National Library exhibition, The People's Treasures, celebrating the efforts of the many individual collectors who have contributed to the enrichment of its holdings in a wide and diverse range of formats.[1] At the same time, that exhibition was designed to draw attention to the strength, variety and character of the many individual collections which have coalesced into the entity, generally referred to in a kind of shorthand as 'the collection'. These brief and prosaic words give no sense of the life and colour of the Library's holdings, no understanding of their range and variety, or their chronological and geographical span and they give no sense of the endeavour, the commitment or the imagination which a succession of individuals brought to the task of shaping and building a collection which is intended to serve the national interest and to reflect the history and values of the peoples who live in Australia and for whom the National Library exists.

John Spiller. Marble medallion portrait of John Webber, c.1790

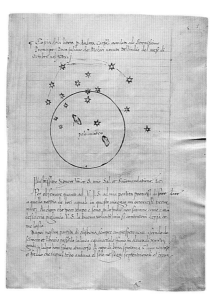

In the context of that exhibition, the word treasures was intended to have a wide and democratic application and, in the words of its curator, to draw attention on the one hand to some of the great icons of our national heritage but on the other to highlight the many things of small individual importance which nevertheless share in a large collective significance. So too in this book, although inevitably the examples selected by individual writers to illustrate their accounts of particular areas of collecting place a premium on qualities such as aesthetic appeal and the related capacity which certain items have to reproduce well and effectively. At the same time, they would argue that their chosen treasures are representative of something that is bigger and more complex. In different ways, each writer is concerned that these items must be seen in context and that they should enable conclusions to be drawn about the nature and purpose of each collecting area.

Other libraries which have sought to represent their collections in volumes which celebrate icons have also been alert to the potential for distortion and misrepresentation of collecting purpose which is implicit in this approach. In 1988 when the British Library published its own 'Treasures' book, the point was carefully made that 'the true treasure of a national library is the collective wisdom of the nation, and its history, its imaginative literature, its laws and commerce, its scientific and technical innovation'.

Readers of the British Library volume were encouraged 'to consider these treasures not just for what they are individually, but as landmarks, among the many other books and documents with which they share space, in the history of the British national library, and, through it, in the history of the nation itself'.[2]

In this same spirit, the treasures which have been identified in this account of the National Library of Australia should be seen as both representative and indicative and, accordingly, they give a sense of the Library's wider holdings and of its national purpose. The collections which make up the whole have been developed for and on behalf of the Australian peoples in all their diversity. At their centre is a great Australian collection which has been consciously constructed to serve as a record of national life and endeavour, to reflect Australian society in all its strengths and weaknesses, in its ethnic and cultural diversity, and to provide the means by which the national memory is nourished and sustained. Side by side with this specialist Australian collection is the Library's extensive holding of overseas materials, which place Australia into its geographic and regional context and provide the link to the wider world community of which Australians are a part.

In a free world, libraries exist as part of the apparatus of a democratic society. They provide access to information, they serve as one of the important conduits for the free exchange of information and ideas and, in the case of state or national libraries, as custodians of the historical record across many disciplines they are an integral part of the cultural environment which they share with other kinds of repositories such as museums, art galleries and archives. Libraries perform many functions: they inform, they educate, they entertain. Inevitably, much goes on behind the scenes which is not visible to the people who use libraries. Much that libraries do is taken for granted. To many they are accepted at face value as mere repositories of books. But what books?—and how and why are they collected? And beyond books, what other forms of record are acquired and why?

To set the scene, Professor Stuart Macintyre provides an eloquent statement of what the National Library has become and how, through its collections, it serves the needs of research and scholarship. As a historian, he properly goes back to the Library's beginnings but his purpose is to place the National Library firmly within its contemporary environment and to see it actively engaged with the Australian society of which it is today an important intellectual and cultural resource. Macintyre offers a scholars' appreciation of the wide range and sweep of, in particular, the Library's Australian collections which exist in many formats—books, newspapers, microforms, paintings, drawings and photographs, music, maps, and oral history interviews and recordings documenting Australia's folk culture and social history. While his chapter acknowledges implicitly the importance of treasures as symbols of a certain role and purpose, his concern is the egalitarian and democratic one to identify the national collection as a resource which has been

developed over time to serve the various needs of the Australian people. The collection has been built to be used and to provide the means by which Australians might better understand themselves, their country and their place in the world.

Macintyre's premise is that a library's collection is its heart or centre. In the National Library of Australia that collection itself—wide-ranging in subject and diverse in format—has its own essential core, the books that form the publishing output of Australia or the books that have been written about Australia and about Australian subjects wherever they have been published. Within that collection again exists another heart, the earliest books about Australia and those that date from the formative years of European settlement and the opening up of the country through inland exploration. Jonathan Wantrup offers an elegant appraisal of some of the Library's outstanding holdings from what may be called the cradle period of Australian books. A distinguished bookseller and himself a noted collector, Wantrup's contribution to this volume reminds us of the debt which libraries of record owe to the antiquarian booktrade.

The partnership which can be forged between libraries and the booktrade will, at its best, be extremely productive and work to the benefit of the collecting institution. Over many years, the National Library in developing and extending its Australian collections, particularly of old and rare materials, has gained substantially from the generosity of a number of outstanding private collectors—Edward Augustus Petherick, Sir John Ferguson, Gregory Macalister Mathews,

Sir Rex Nan Kivell and Ronald Vere Tooley to name a few. But no less important has been the relationship maintained with the antiquarian book trade. In Australia, dealers such as Peter Arnold, Leo Berkelouw, Kenneth Hince, Anne McCormick and Derek McDonnell of Hordern House, Tim McCormick, Nicholas Pounder, Michael Treloar and a number of others have each, in various ways, offered a singular service to the Library which has been predicated upon a sense of the central place it occupies as a great national repository of Australian materials. That same spirit of courtesy and generosity expressed so freely by the booktrade in Australia has also been forthcoming from a number of distinguished bookselling houses overseas. Pre-eminent among these are the London firms of Maggs Bros and Bernard Quaritch. The National Library's association with these two firms extends back over almost the whole of the past century.

Developed alongside its Australian book collections, and for almost as long a period, is the Library's rich collection of the personal papers of Australian men and women together with the papers of a wide range of nationally important organisations. The remarkable diversity of these collections over many fields of endeavour, together with complementary holdings of oral history, folkloric and social history recordings, have contributed to the Library's reputation and standing as one of the great centres of research about Australian life and achievement, particularly in the period since Federation. The genesis of this collection and the story of its remarkable growth and development is told by Graeme Powell who, with other library staff over many years, has contributed significantly to its present standing.

In Australia, the great libraries of record such as the National Library of Australia, the State Library of New South Wales and the State Library of Victoria have all recognised that their archival and documentary role embraces visual representations of various kinds. They have a strong tradition in collecting a wide range of pictorial materials—historical and topographic paintings, portraits, drawings and other works on paper, posters and photographs. It is interesting that as a result of the recognition by such libraries that pictorial materials served an important documentary purpose, some of the most outstanding colonial art collections which exist in the public domain in Australia do so in libraries. While the relative neglect by art museums in this field in earlier years has been balanced by the development of more inclusive collecting programs which today acknowledge the critical formative importance of Australian colonial art, the National Library in common with a number of state libraries, continues to recognise that such material is capable of a variety of readings and of use. That special interest and purpose is addressed in this book by Dr Sasha Grishin.

Another form of the documentary record is provided in maps and charts. The National Library's remarkable strength in this field, particularly the concentration which has been given to the mapping of Australia, is reviewed by Associate Professor Terry Birtles. While admitting the aesthetic and decorative appeal of maps, especially those which date from the sixteenth and seventeenth centuries, Birtles' purpose is the more serious one to place maps into context as documents to be read, used and interpreted to better understand the nature and achievements of human enterprise in various forms. His overview of the National Library's map holdings ranges historically from the earliest known depictions of the antipodean world to the late twentieth century when maps embody a rich mass of social information.

If at the centre of this book is the National Library's preoccupation with things Australian, also important has been its concern to collect materials which acknowledge Australia's place in its specific geographic region. A wider cultural frame again is provided in those collections which acknowledge a cultural debt to the traditions of European and fine book production, and to the great humanitarian traditions of scholarship and debate.

Two essays deal with this extended arena of collecting. Andrew Gosling explores the extensive Asian collections which today underpin and reflect an increasingly dynamic relationship between Australia and the countries of the Asia–Pacific region. It is important also to acknowledge the cultural value which these materials represent for those Australians who trace their ancestry back to the various countries of this region. Margaret Dent offers a graceful account of the Library's Rare Books collection and

in so doing acknowledges those forces of modernity which broke the chains of the medieval world and set in train the revolution which transformed book production and, therefore, the means for the wide dissemination and communication of ideas. The changes wrought by that revolution have continued to exert their influence late into the twentieth century. On the threshold of a new century, computer technology offers a further dramatic refinement to the mass communication of ideas and information which was Johann Gutenberg's legacy to the world.

This book celebrates the collection which has been accumulated by the National Library over a period of almost one hundred years. The building of that collection has owed much to the support provided by successive Australian governments; it has also owed immeasurably to the genius, dedication and generosity of individual collectors both large and small, who have contributed texture and depth to the collection; it has benefited from the assistance provided by the booktrade; and it has been influenced by the work of several generations of library staff who have worked to interpret the collecting mandate as it has changed and evolved over the years. This work continues—collecting, processing, organising materials for use and ensuring their preservation and survival for future generations. These tasks require a sensitivity to that brief which is the special preserve of libraries of record to ensure the best possible documentation of the societies which it is their job to serve. This book honours the adherence to that tradition which has been the work of the National Library of Australia and which will guide it in the years ahead.

PEOPLE'S TREASURES, PEOPLE'S HISTORY: USING AND INTERPRETING THE NATIONAL COLLECTION

Stuart Macintyre

You can see them every morning on the podium overlooking the Lake as they wait for the Library to open, their breath pluming the winter air. They are not the casual visitors, for those come later with the tourist buses. These pilgrims carry pencils and notebooks, or perhaps a portable computer; some are eager and some preoccupied, their thoughts already turning to the work they left the night before. These are the scholars, the researchers for whom the holdings of the National Library are a precious resource.

There will be more of them in the summer, when the end of the academic year allows more time for the trip to Canberra. Some will make use of the Library at a distance, by interlibrary loan or through its Australian Bibliographic Network, while for others the Library offers a gateway to further collections elsewhere in Australia and beyond.

But for all who enter the building and make their way to its various service points—the Main Reading Room and the Petherick Room on the ground floor; the newspaper section, the oral history corner and the map room on the floor below, as well as the various specialist collections above—there is that pleasurable anticipation of handling familiar objects and the sharp excitement of discovering new ones. Such regular users are by no means the only concern of the Library, yet they enjoy a special relationship with it because of their absorption: they write and publish, interpret and reinterpret what they find. With words and images they project the Library's collection outwards to wider circles of readers.

At the heart of every library there is a collection, an accumulation of books and records and other materials that is a living record of the purposes that library has served. A national library serves a variety of purposes: users come to it with very different needs and the collecting policy necessarily responds to changing circumstances. It can benefit from munificence or suffer from neglect, seize opportunities or lose them, and the results will be apparent to future generations. For a national library necessarily operates both for the present and for posterity. Its collection is a sedimentary record of how the nation was conceived and of the shifting understandings of the national heritage.

The origins of the National Library of Australia lie in the formation of a federal union nearly a hundred years ago. When they gathered in Melbourne in 1901 the members of the new Commonwealth Parliament established a library committee to serve their needs and straightaway

The Petherick Reading Room, named after the collector E.A. Petherick, is one of several specialist reading rooms in the National Library used for long-term scholarly research

Captain James Cook's *Endeavour* journal with *Doncker's Zee-Atlas* and the marine callipers thought to have been used by William Dampier

fell to discussion of its scope and purpose. Some wanted no more than a working reference library for legislators, such as they found in the library of the Victorian Parliament whose guests they were and would remain for a quarter of a century. Such a facility would acquire popular literature and periodicals for members to borrow, works of record for them to consult, and might also hold curiosa such as the book in the Parliament House strongroom bound in the human skin of victims guillotined in the French Revolution. But as the Prime Minister, Edmund Barton, suggested, the chief test should be practical utility and the library would have a 'specific & eclectic character'.[1]

At the other extreme lay the vision of the chairman of that committee and first speaker of the House of Representatives, Sir Frederick Holder, who had in mind a Library of a 'general and comprehensive' character that would be worthy of the Australian nation:

> the home of the literature, not of a State, or of a period, but of the world, and of all time; a centre to which may gravitate as years pass, manuscripts and other documents and records of all kinds whatever, relating to the discovery, colonization, history, and development of Australia and its adjacent regions.[2]

The obstacles to achievement of this grand ideal were considerable. The Commonwealth Parliamentary Library lacked staff and resources;

it had no adequate repository; many of the rarest heritage items had already been acquired by that extraordinary bibliophile David Scott Mitchell and recently passed to the then Public Library in Sydney.

Yet in the early decades there were clear steps to establish a national collection. In 1909 the Commonwealth acquired a major collection of Australiana from E.A. Petherick (confirmed by Act of Parliament in 1911), in 1912 it legislated a new Copyright Act to enforce the deposit of all new Australian publications, in the same year it engaged Dr Frederick Watson to edit the *Historical Records of Australia*. If the Melbourne Public Library still commanded the largest collection of printed materials and the Mitchell Library was still adding to its manuscript collection with the papers of Governor Macquarie and Bligh's *Bounty* log, then the Commonwealth prevailed in 1923 when it bought Cook's *Endeavour* journal. This coup justified the renaming of the Australian section of the Parliamentary Library as the Commonwealth National Library; and while the collection was still not open to general access—not in Melbourne and not in Canberra when the library followed the parliamentarians there in 1927—the Library Committee rejoiced that it was already being used by students of Australian history.[3]

The slow metamorphosis continued. A separate National Library building opened in Canberra in 1935. The National Library was established in its own right, by statute in 1960, and then in 1968 settled into its present location on the shores of Lake Burley Griffin. Each stage in the institutional process, each enlargement of facilities and provisions followed the insistent tug of the growing national collection. Its creators willed the National Library of Australia into being by their acquisitions.

Even in the 1920s, there were clear indications of the judgement that was shaping the collection. While the Library exercised its right to receive Australian publications very selectively, rejecting whole categories of literature such as children's books, it persuaded the Commonwealth to outlay large sums for special purchases such as Ellis Rowan's paintings of flowers and Hardy Wilson's drawings of Australian historic buildings. From the 1940s began the transfer of Sir John Ferguson's notable collection of books, manuscripts and pictures, completed after his death in 1969 by the purchase of the remainder. In 1948 that exotic New Zealand-born art dealer Rex Nan Kivell gave the Library custody of part of his extraordinarily rich pictorial and literary record of the early history of Australia, New Zealand and the Pacific; it was bought in 1959 with a further major instalment being given to the Library over a period of years.[4] In the same spirit the Library bought one of the original copies of the *Magna Carta*, along with other medieval works.

These acquisitions were valued for their rarity and aesthetic qualities, their richness as a scholarly resource but most of all for their emblematic cultural significance. They codified a particular kind of national endeavour and achievement, the apprehension and possession of the island-continent in the south-west Pacific. Ernest Scott, the great scientific romancer of discovery and settlement, and Professor of History at the University of Melbourne, said of Hardy Wilson's drawings when the federal

Terrestrial globe
dated 1814, by
W. & J.M. Bardin

Treasurer begrudged their price that in a century they would be absolutely priceless.[5] Foresight and hindsight linked colonial beginnings, backwards to its cultural heritage and forwards to national destiny. By assembling such rarities, the custodians defined the collection as a permanent record of visionary achievement.

Both complementing and also tempering that understanding of a national collection, was the growing weight attached to research. The Australian Joint Copying Project began as a logical sequel to the *Historical Records of Australia* with the object of filming archival material relevant to Australia held in British repositories. It commenced in 1945 as a joint venture with the Mitchell Library, concentrating on the vast holdings of the Public Record Office in London, but then expanding with the arrival of Phyllis Mander-Jones. Her pursuit of private records led in 1972 to the publication of *Manuscripts in the British Isles Relating to Australia, New Zealand, and the Pacific,* and today the Project has yielded nearly 10 000 reels of microfilm amounting to five million pages of records.[6] Watson had described his edited selection of *Historical Records* as 'the birth certificates of a nation':[7] for scores of present-day researchers, those images on the screen of the microfilm reader are a necessary device for the production of knowledge.

In the same spirit, there was the acquisition in the 1960s of the Nichol Smith collection of English literature, an extremely strong resource of Restoration and eighteenth-century rare editions. Such materials extended the range and depth of Australian learning, allowing scholars based in Australia to conduct important research and attracting scholars from abroad to work here.

Thus the National Library sustained the work of the Australian universities during the post-war decades as they adapted to the research imperative. But the continued expansion of higher education has brought with it an expansion of its own library provision; today the university libraries have become cuckoos in the public library nest, expending many times the sum available to the National and state libraries for their acquisitions. The National Library has had to modify that grand aspiration of Sir Frederick Holder—'the home of the literature, not of a State or a period, but of the world, and of all time'—for not even the Library of Congress in America can today hope to collect on that munificent scale.

In any case, the establishment of other national collecting agencies, the Australian War Memorial, the Australian Archives, the National Gallery of Australia, the National Film and Sound Archive, the Australian Institute of Aboriginal and Torres Strait Islander Studies, the Australian National Maritime Museum and even the fledgling National Museum of Australia, has necessarily redefined the scope of the Library's activity. The Library has accommodated these partners, lending generously to exhibitions, making adjustments to its collecting policy to acknowledge the special collecting responsibilities of others, and

Alfred Deakin's diaries for 1902 and 1903, with his 1890 Federation Conference folder sometimes placing materials elsewhere or transferring functions. Recognising the outstanding artistic importance of a number of key paintings in its collection, the Library has negotiated a special long-term lending arrangement with its near neighbour, the National Gallery of Australia.

The national collection continues to span books and manuscripts, maps and music, newspapers and illustrative material, the spoken as well as the written voice, that record the lives and activities of notable Australians. Perhaps the most significant trend over the recent past has been to broaden the reach of the collection from the notable and the institutional to the popular and inclusive. The Library has become less grandly monumental in its understanding of its national role.

As a monocultural has yielded to a multicultural Australia, there has been a determined effort to acquire material that illustrates social and ethnic diversity. For example, the papers of Arthur Calwell are a particularly rich source on post-war immigration policy. Papers that document the careers of such prominent individuals as Daisy Bates, Jane Franklin, Enid Lyons, Jean Macnamara, Nellie Melba, Nettie Palmer, Katharine Susannah Prichard, Ruby Rich, Henry Handel Richardson and Jessie Street, and more recently Robyn Archer, are complemented by the records that show women engaged together in various enterprises; the Country Women's Association, the Women Pilots Association and the Women's Electoral Lobby. The established holdings on Aboriginal missions are joined by newer collections where the

Aboriginal and Torres Strait Islanders speak for themselves. Recent acquisitions of the papers of Kevin Gilbert, Sally Morgan and Charles Perkins are noteworthy examples.

During the early operation of the Copyright Act, the Library had little interest in ephemera: the Librarian was explicitly instructed to destroy 'race-track programmes' and other such 'worthless matter'.[8] By 1960 the National Library Act laid down a responsibility to develop 'a comprehensive collection of library materials relating to Australia and the Australian people'. And even that formulation has taken on a larger meaning as both scholars and librarians have relaxed prescriptive definitions of cultural significance. In particular, the growing fascination with the popular, and the shift of historical consciousness from the monumental to the lived experience, has reshaped recent collecting practices.

This is especially apparent in the Library's Oral History collection, which began with the pioneer endeavours of Hazel de Berg. From 1957 to 1984 she recorded over 1200 interviews with notable Australians, beginning with writers and artists and moving on to composers, actors, academics, scientists, public servants and politicians.[9] Any of the latter who felt aggrieved by their omission were more than compensated by the Parliament's Oral History Project, which was one by-product of the bicentennial urge to record and allowed federal parliamentarians to speak as long as their voice lasted—some of the bound transcriptions, which were copied for the National Library, defy even the most muscular user to lump onto a reading table in one trip from the issuing desk.

While the Library's oral history program still records eminent Australians, it now takes in the lives of people seen as representative of groups in Australian society: trade unionists, the unemployed, the Chinese, Australians with AIDS. It also has particular strength in folklore, supplementing the priceless material recorded by John Meredith in the 1950s with subsequent recordings of folk in many cultures. Here, as in other parts of the collection, an extended appreciation of the vernacular bends back to meet an augmented awareness of difference and diversity.

Those who make use of the collections can easily overlook just what is involved in assembling them. Take one of the jewels of the manuscript collection, the papers of Alfred Deakin. Both as a notable public figure—the most visionary of the federal fathers as well as prime minister—and as an intensely private figure who was constantly setting down his inner thoughts, Deakin created a large body of material. After he died, his son-in-law Herbert Brookes organised the papers for Walter Murdoch, Deakin's first biographer in the early 1920s. Twenty years later, after protracted

Hardy Wilson.
George's Hall,
George's River,
N.S.W., 1916

negotiation, Brookes acceded in 1945 to the request of the Library, backed by a letter from Prime Minister Curtin, that the papers might eventually come to the Library. But it took another two decades of anxious waiting, and the completion of another biography by the historian John La Nauze, before Brookes' widow finally presented the papers. They are now secure and available to researchers, complete with a detailed guide and substantial additional material provided by La Nauze—and the further riches of the papers of Herbert and Ivy Brookes. No serious scholar of public and intellectual life in the early Commonwealth ignores them.[10]

Consider those who have used those papers. Apart from La Nauze, who mined them afresh for his study of *The Making of the Australian Constitution*, Al Gabay made them the basis of his exploration of *The Mystic Life of Alfred Deakin*, while Jill Roe wove them into her evocative account of theosophy in Australia, *Beyond Belief*. Laurie Fitzhardinge counterposed them with the papers of William Morris Hughes, Deakin's Labor adversary, and the papers of various other politicians, also in the National Library, to write his biography of the Little Digger. John Rickard set them against the papers of H.B. Higgins and other contemporaries to illuminate the emergence of class politics in the Commonwealth, as too did Peter Loveday, Allan Martin and R.S. Parker in their consideration of *The Emergence of the Australian Party System*. And Manning Clark employed his idiosyncratic eye to bring Mr Deakin so insistently into volume five of the grand *History of Australia*.

Working alongside them, as they pieced together these chains of correspondence and made out allusions in scrawled diary entries, were other scholars. There was the New Zealander, John Beaglehole, conning the journals of James Cook for his superb biography, there was Dorothy Green, at work on her study of Henry Handel Richardson, and Ann Moyal charting the history of Australian science. There was the young Humphrey McQueen, skirmishing against the radical nationalist legend, and the doyen of Australian historians, Sir Keith Hancock, working in his autumnal years on the natural history of the Monaro. There was Henry Reynolds, piecing together fragments of the other side of the frontier, and David Marr, tracing out the life of Patrick White. The correspondence of Nettie Palmer is pivotal to Drusilla Modjeska's account of women writers of the interwar years, *Exiles at Home*, while Carole Ferrier has quarried the collection for her work on one of these writers, Jean Devanny.

Major collaborative enterprises have drawn heavily on the Library's collections. For ten years the team assembled by Bill Ramson at the Australian National University combed holdings of rare Australian imprints for examples of local usage in order to create *The Australian National Dictionary*. The lifespan of the *Australian Dictionary of Biography* stretches over three decades and still its researchers make their way across the Lake from their base in the H.C. Coombs Building to piece together details of men and women whose records were deposited in the National Library. For the lavishly illustrated bicentennial series *Australians: A Historical Library* extensive use was made of the Library's collections.

These and other scholars in other fields of study—Australian literature and the fine arts, business history and the history of science, sport and topography, Asia and the Antarctic, the performing arts and public administration, philately and folk culture, linguistics and the law—all have recourse to the collections of the National Library.

Those collections have been assembled, organised and maintained by the staff of the Library on behalf of the nation. There are strengths and weaknesses. Sometimes an item was secured by patient courtship, sometimes it got away. Finite resources and circumstantial judgements have shaped the collection, and will shape it into the future. Rather than lament the absences—for how could that utopian impossibility, the complete national collection, ever provide the thrill of discovery?—we celebrate them as the palpable expression of restless human endeavour in our part of the world.

THE HEART OF THE MATTER: KEEPING THE BOOKS OF AUSTRALIA

Jonathan Wantrup

Each of the many thousand or more Australian books in the National Library of Australia is in its own way a treasure. Together they form a detailed mosaic of our nation's past and present, recording the passions and struggles, the successes and failures, imaginings and expectations of the generations of men and women who sought to draw the outline of Terra Australis on the map and, later, who sought to fulfil their destiny within its shores.

As the central repository of our national heritage, as a 'library of last resort', the Library's comprehensive collection of Australiana is necessarily rich. If it is true that as a nation we place a special emphasis on the individual, then it is fitting that this richness should be founded on the uncommon enthusiasm of four individual collectors: the pioneering bibliographer, E.A. Petherick; the great ornithologist, Gregory Macalister Mathews; the outstanding collector and our national bibliographer, Sir John Ferguson; and the art dealer and distinguished collector, Sir Rex Nan Kivell.

The Petherick collection has been described as 'the nucleus of the National Library's collection of materials relating to Australia and the Pacific'.[1] A bookman to his bootstraps, Petherick was bookseller, bibliographer, antiquarian cataloguer, voracious collector and—appropriately—a bankrupt. Through it all he assembled a magnificent collection of over 15 000 books,

pamphlets, maps and pictures relating to Australasia that was formally acquired by Act of Parliament in 1911. To this solid foundation were added the fine Mathews ornithological collection in 1939; between 1937 and Sir John's death in 1969, the 34 000 items that make up the rich and diverse Ferguson collection; and, finally, the extraordinary Nan Kivell collection recording the early history of Australasia and the Pacific through well over 10 000 books, manuscripts, topographical works of art, prints and photographs formally acquired in 1959. The Nan Kivell collection was a remarkable acquisition, providing a quantum leap in the Library's already strong collections of these materials. As an art dealer, Sir Rex brought to his collecting a highly developed connoisseurship and a clearly defined sense of purpose that gave his assemblage of superficially quite diverse materials a remarkable integrity and coherence.

It would, however, be very misleading to give the impression that the Library's great strength relied entirely on these impressive private collections. The Library has itself for many decades been an energetic collector, and not only can that 'collection' stand shoulder to shoulder with each of the Petherick, Mathews, Ferguson and Nan Kivell collections but, in some respects, it surpasses them. The Library's role as the national library of record also means that books of Australian interest published throughout the world are acquired—resources permitting—upon publication. As well, by law, a deposit copy of every book published in the Commonwealth of Australia must be provided, thus ensuring that the books of this century—the printed treasures of the future—are preserved and recorded as they wait upon the judgement of our descendants.

The story of the Australian book, like the history of European Australia, begins well before a white man ever set foot on Australian shores. Ancient geographers had speculated about the existence of a vast continent to the south and medieval writers and travellers such as Marco Polo retailed very garbled accounts of a vast and rich land. When Magellan entered the Pacific around Cape Horn in 1520, the likelihood increased that Terra Australis would be found within its waters. So did the speculation and theorising. Indeed, it was as late as 1774 that James Cook firmly laid the theory of the Great Southern Continent to rest by sailing right over a large portion of it.

Sailing from Europe around Africa to the spice-rich East in the sixteenth and seventeenth centuries, mercantile Dutch sea captains were several times blown off course and, literally, bumped into the coast of western Australia. From their foothold in Batavia Dutch officials made forays to the coasts of the Southland, by then known as New Holland. Many of those who made these first accidental contacts and explorations—or sent them out—have left their names on the map: Houtman, Carpentier, Nuyts, Van Diemen, Tasman and Hartog, among others.

The Dutch left printed records of some of these voyages, unlike the Portuguese and Spanish who may also have stumbled on Terra Australis. It was not until Pedro de Queiros, a Portuguese in the service of Spain, set off in 1605 from Callao in Peru west across the Pacific in search of Terra Australis that any work concerning the search for the Southland was published in those great seafaring empires. Even then, the Spanish memorials reporting Queiros's expedition and urging a continuation were printed virtually in secrecy and in very limited numbers. The English were equally slow. It is ironic that the first English

Engraved plates from *Ongeluckige Voyagie, van 't Schip Batavia, nae de Oost-Indien* by the explorer Francisco Pelsaert, showing the *Batavia* and the aftermath of a mutiny

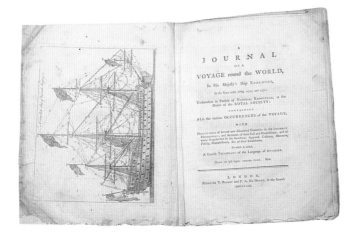

book relating to the discovery of Australia was a translation of de Queiros's Spanish memorial published in London in 1617. It was not until the end of the seventeenth century that William Dampier became the first Englishman to set foot on Australia. He visited New Holland twice, in 1688 and 1699, and published popular and often reprinted accounts of those voyages in 1697 and 1703. Early printed accounts of all these voyages are held in the National Library: in most cases these are the uniformly rare early editions, although there are still some gaps to fill.

One of the rarest—and certainly one of the most sensational—is the 1647 first edition of Francisco Pelsaert's account of the wreck of the large Dutch East India Company ship, *Batavia*, off the western coast of Australia in 1629. After the *Batavia* ran aground, Pelsaert and a small crew had set off east in search of a mainland, leaving nearly 300 survivors on two islands. A bloody mutiny broke out among part of the crew, who murdered and raped the civilian survivors indiscriminately.

Meanwhile Pelsaert, unsuccessful in his search for fresh water on the mainland, sailed north to the settlement at Batavia, in the process becoming the first European to discover a long stretch of the west coast. The mutineers surrendered when Pelsaert returned with a new ship. He tried them and hanged most of them on gallows erected on the mainland. Two others he marooned there, thus bringing European justice to Australian shores and commencing a tradition of dumping criminals in Australia that was to be enthusiastically embraced by the English over 150 years later.

Pelsaert's narrative of his arduous journey became the first printed account of a voyage of Australian discovery and the somewhat macabre engravings of murder and execution are the first published depictions of any part of the Australian continent.

Despite these discoveries on the west and north coasts by the Dutch, it was not until the end of the next century that the east coast, and consequently the overall outline of the continent was known. The first voyage of Captain James Cook in HMS *Endeavour*, complemented by his two subsequent voyages, established the general conformation of the Pacific, for the first time laying open to European geography the outline of Australia and New Zealand, and the existence of many Pacific islands, most notably Hawaii. Cook's voyages marked a turning point in the history of European man's understanding of the globe when he demonstrated the non-existence of the antipodean counterpoise, the Great Southern Continent of ancient, medieval and modern speculation.

The Library not only holds copies of the official accounts of Cook's voyages but the unofficial and surreptitious accounts as well. The British Admiralty insisted that all members of an expedition hand over their logs upon their return, so that the official account of the voyage might not be pre-empted. This was no oppressive monopoly: it was one way to reward the commander of an expedition who usually received a portion of royalties. The interest and importance of Cook's voyages meant, however, that there was a strong financial incentive to breach this embargo and so it is that in each case a surreptitious, and invariably anonymous, unofficial account appeared first. The earliest published account of the discovery of the east coast of Australia, for instance, was published in London two months after the return of the *Endeavour* in 1771 and two years before the official account. That anonymous volume, titled *A Journal of a Voyage Round the World in His Majesty's Ship* Endeavour, is generally attributed to the American loyalist sailor, James Magra. The London publishers, Becket and de Hondt, very cheekily dedicated the volume to 'The Right Honourable Lords of the Admiralty, and to Mr. Banks and Dr. Solander'. Legal action was swiftly taken against the publisher and the leaf bearing this unauthorised dedication was removed from

most copies. Those that still retain this leaf are now very rare and much prized.

Such was the contemporary fame of James Cook and the abiding interest of his discoveries that his voyages generated a vast quantity of books, pamphlets and engravings. Among the Library's extensive collection of Cook material are virtually all the important contemporary printed works. These range from surgeon David Samwell's sober, very rare and highly important eyewitness account of Cook's violent death, published in London in 1786, to Alexander Shaw's equally rare and delightfully eccentric 1787 *A Catalogue of the Different Specimens of Cloth Collected in the Three Voyages of Captain Cook*, comprising a printed text and thirty-nine specimens of cloth. The copy in the Ferguson collection has an additional complement making a total of over fifty specimens.

For Australians, the most important consequence of Cook's discoveries was the 1786 proposal to establish a settlement in New South Wales. Actively debated at the time, it was not greeted with universal approval. Cook's old adversary, the hydrographer Alexander Dalrymple, strongly opposed the plan—probably from personal motives—and published in 1786 what is now an extremely rare *Serious Admonition to the Publick, on the Intended Thief-Colony at Botany Bay*. Others opposed the use of convicts as settlers upon humanitarian grounds, such as the anonymous 'G.R' who published *Proposals, for Employing Convicts, within this Kingdom; Instead of Sending Them to Botany Bay* to argue his case. The Library's copy of that rare 1787 pamphlet is the only one held in an Australian library.

PORT JACKSON SHARK.

A Poto Roo

In the end, Governor Arthur Phillip's First Fleet was sent across the world to establish a European presence in the new continent. This fleet constituted the largest movement of ships into the Pacific and the most significant act of long-distance migration ever undertaken. Public interest in the enterprise was intense and many accounts of the First Fleet voyage and the early days of the settlement were published in the years after 1788. The earliest published account, based on interviews with the crews of returning vessels, was written by an English journalist using the pseudonym of 'An Officer'. The first genuine eyewitness account of the new settlement at Port Jackson was published a few weeks later. It was written by Watkin Tench, a lieutenant of Marines, and went through four editions in London and Dublin and many translations within a year. His was also the earliest account of New South Wales published in the United States. The Library's copy of the extremely rare 1789 New York edition of Tench's book, the only one known in Australia, is one of the many treasures acquired by the Library in more recent years as it builds on the foundations of Petherick, Ferguson and Nan Kivell.

As soon as the first marquees and huts were set up in Sydney Cove, Governor Phillip began the task of exploring the hinterland and surveying Sydney Harbour and the adjacent coast. These earliest expeditions are recorded in the various publications of the First Fleet diarists. Within a decade more extensive expeditions by land and sea were being undertaken. Progressive exploration continued for over a century: even today there are still portions of the continent yet to be thoroughly explored and the task of charting the coastline in refined detail continues with the aid of satellite technology.

Perhaps it says something about us as a nation that many of the most significant discoveries were first broadcast, often as an afterthought, in more or less humble format, in limited numbers and with poor distribution. *Observations on the Coasts of Van Diemen's Land*, Matthew Flinders' account of the voyage in which he established for the first time that Tasmania was an island, was published in 1801 at the author's expense in very limited numbers in London. Gregory Blaxland's *Journal of a Tour of Discovery across the Blue Mountains* was published ten years after the event in 1823 in London and then in such limited numbers that it appears to have been purely a private publication for family use. An even greater delay occurred with Hamilton Hume's account of the discovery of the rich lands around Port Phillip in 1824–25. Hume's own narrative of this expedition, which he led in fact if not in name, was not published until May 1855. As with the books of Flinders and Blaxland, the first printing of Hume's *Brief Statement* is very rare: the Ferguson

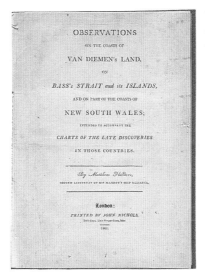

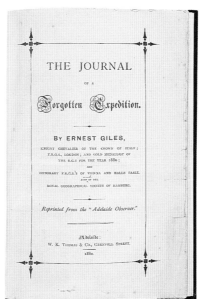

copy in the National Library is the only one known. Ernest Giles, 'the last of the explorers', felt strongly enough to title one of his narratives *The Journal of a Forgotten Expedition*. Published in 1880 in limited numbers, this was privately distributed by the explorer and is now so rare that the book, like the achievements of its author, has been largely forgotten. It is a salutary reminder of how easily overlooked great deeds might be without the collectors and libraries who preserve these books.

The story of our nation is not, however, merely the story of great deeds. It is pre-eminently the story of how ordinary men and women came over the seas to make their homes in this strange antipodean land. It is also the story of how the newcomers displaced and depleted, often without malice, the original inhabitants.

Despite the pseudo-scientific curiosity that they inspired in contemporary Europe, the Aborigines are not very well served by the early published record. The earliest serious attempt to record and publish details of the lives of the Sydney tribes will be found in an appendix to Colonel David Collins' 1798 *Account of the English Colony*, illustrated by engravings after Thomas Watling, the convict artist. The first separate

The title page of *Observations on the Coasts of Van Diemen's Land, on Bass's Strait and Its Islands and on Part of the Coasts of New South Wales...* by the distinguished explorer and navigator Matthew Flinders

The Journal of a Forgotten Expedition by Ernest Giles

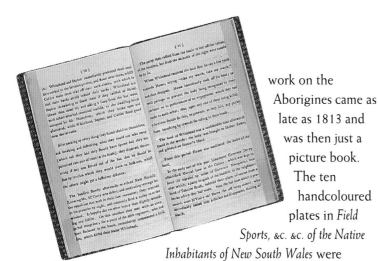

work on the Aborigines came as late as 1813 and was then just a picture book. The ten handcoloured plates in *Field Sports, &c. &c. of the Native Inhabitants of New South Wales* were engraved after drawings by the English artist John Heaviside Clark. Clark had never visited New South Wales and his illustrations were based on drawings made in the colony, possibly by the artist John William Lewin. The first Australian-printed works on the Aborigines were not published until 1827–28, when the missionary Lancelot Threlkeld published two pamphlets about his work among the already demoralised original inhabitants. Even more shameful, we have to leap a century before the first published work by an Aborigine makes an appearance: David Unaipon's *Native Legends*.

The most enthralling and frequently the scarcest of the personal accounts written by the first 'New Australians' are those written by and about convicts. Although later historians glossed over the 'unseemly' past, the role of convicts in early colonial life was considerable. Australia's pioneering printer, George Howe, was a convict; the first artists were convicts; the first local historian was a convict, John Slater, whose *Description of Sydney* was printed in 1819; the first book printed in Tasmania was an account of the death of the escaped convict and bushranger, Mike Howe. Dozens of other convict narratives,

almost invariably cheaply printed pamphlets and broadsides, were issued during the period of transportation. The National Library has an exceptional collection of these biographies and autobiographies, in some cases—the 1818 Hobart account of Mike Howe is an example— holding copies unique in Australia.

After a century of European occupation it was not convicts nor Aborigines who made up the largest group in Australian society. Free emigration had started slowly in the colony but by the end of the 1820s was in full swing. While the promoters were often men who had never left Europe, people within the colony began to sing its praises in published 'descriptions' and 'guides' for emigrants. Among the most notable of them were Australian-born statesman William Charles

One of ten coloured plates by John Heaviside Clark from his *Field Sports, &c. &c. of the Native Inhabitants of New South Wales*. The engraver was M. Dubourg

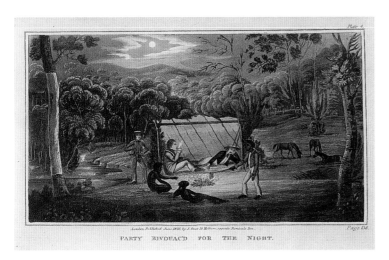

PARTY BIVOUACD FOR THE NIGHT.

An aquatint from *An Account of the State of Agriculture & Grazing in New South Wales* by James Atkinson

Wentworth, explorer and bookseller George William Evans, company agent Edward Curr, and farmer James Atkinson, who not only published the first account of Australian agriculture in 1826 but also fathered Australia's first woman novelist, Louisa Atkinson, and was married to the author of the first Australian children's book, Charlotte Barton.

Within thirty years new colonies had sprung up in Western Australia, South Australia, Victoria and Queensland. Emigration had found its English champions in Edward Gibbon Wakefield, Samuel and John Sidney, Alexander Harris and Caroline Chisholm. It was, however, the gold rushes that produced the greatest surge in emigration and the greatest flood of promotional literature. It is extraordinary how many diggers—and usually failed ones at that— returned to their towns and villages throughout Great Britain and continental Europe and promptly published guides to the Australian diggings, often eccentrically printed by unskilled provincial printers and now of considerable rarity.

The Californian and Australian gold rushes produced the most extensive mass movement of men and women ever seen, and it is the special quality of these rough-hewn diggers' accounts that they tell that story from the ordinary person's point of view.

From the earliest days of European settlement the colonists' hands were turned not just to labour with pick and shovel but to the practice of the arts and sciences. Convict artists, almost invariably highly skilled forgers, and amateur military artists recorded the birds, animals, plants and landscape of

A Mountain Bee-eater, one of many delicate illustrations in John Lewin's *Birds of New Holland...* 1808

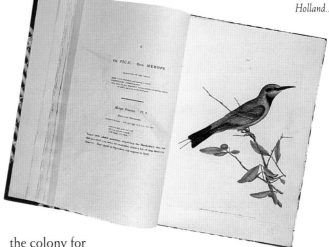

the colony for transmission to scientists in Europe. The first professional artist to work in Australia, for example, was the natural history artist John William Lewin. In 1813 Lewin had printed in Sydney his now rare and valuable *Birds of New South Wales* illustrated with his handcoloured engravings. This was the first work produced for general publication in the colony. The National Library holds a copy of this 1813 volume and its

21

even rarer predecessor, the 1808 London-printed *Birds of New Holland*, which survives in less than ten copies. It is due to the presumed loss of the remaining copies of this 1808 first edition that we believe Lewin published his Sydney version five years later.

It is Lewin's personal connection with Australia that earns him first mention but his work was not the earliest illustrated account of the continent's 'natural productions'. In 1793–94 Sir James Smith and George Shaw began publication of a fine series describing the botany and zoology of New South Wales. They began a tradition of superbly illustrated Australian natural history books that culminates in the work of Ferdinand Bauer, John Gould, Silvester Diggles and, in this century, Gregory Macalister Mathews.

In the same year that Lewin published his Sydney book, an enterprising ex-convict, Absalom West, employed convict artists to engrave a series of Sydney landscapes. A very rare series, this was the first Australian topographical view book. Until the general decline in engraving caused by the spread of photography in the 1870s, many such series of engraved views were published in Australia and England. Arguably the rarest is the set of *Views in Australia* published by

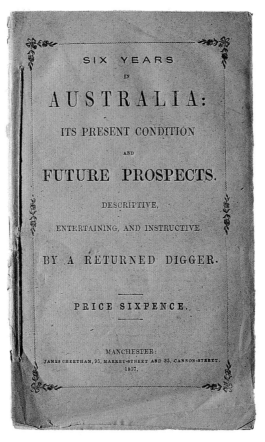

SIX YEARS
IN
AUSTRALIA:

ITS PRESENT CONDITION
AND
FUTURE PROSPECTS.

DESCRIPTIVE,

ENTERTAINING, AND INSTRUCTIVE.

BY A RETURNED DIGGER.

PRICE SIXPENCE.

MANCHESTER:
JAMES CHEETHAM, 95, MARKET-STREET AND 33, CANNON-STREET.
1857.

Augustus Earle in Sydney in 1826. This was the earliest example of lithography produced in the colony and one of the most beautiful Australian colourplate books ever produced. For many years the Nan Kivell copy in the National Library was the only one recorded.

It is surely no coincidence that Lewin and West produced their artistic and scientific works in the age of Macquarie, the civilising governor. So it is that the first Australian poets, Michael Massey Robinson and Judge Barron Field, produced their work under his patronage. Robinson, an attorney convicted of forgery, wrote the first poems published in Australia between 1811 and 1821. His work was, however, only published in the *Sydney Gazette* and as broadsheets. The first 'book' of poetry published here was written by the Supreme Court judge, Barron Field, a close friend of Charles Lamb and his circle. His *First Fruits of Australian Poetry* was published in Sydney in 1819, with a second edition in 1823. It is of such great rarity that one pious story has it that as David Scott Mitchell lay on his death-bed his bookseller pressed a recently discovered copy of Field's slim volume into his dying hands. The copy in the National Library is aptly paired with a copy of the

1823 second edition. This latter has special interest since it is inscribed by the poet to Samuel Taylor Coleridge. Both of these volumes were Petherick's, a neat demonstration of the riches of his collection.

As a taste of the rich record of our literary heritage preserved in the Library, other literary firsts include the first work by an Australian-born poet (William Charles Wentworth's *Australasia*, published London 1823), the first book of poetry published in Australia by an Australian-born poet (Charles Tompson's *Wild Notes, from the Lyre of a Native Minstrel*, published Sydney 1826), the first Australian novel (convict Henry Savery's *Quintus Servinton*, published Hobart and London, 1830–32), and the first Australian children's book (Charlotte Barton's *A Mother's Offering to Her Children*, published Sydney 1841).

With such foundations to build on, the task of the National Library today is to seek material that extends the themes developed in the great formed collections of Petherick, Ferguson, Nan Kivell, Mathews and others. Above all, the Library

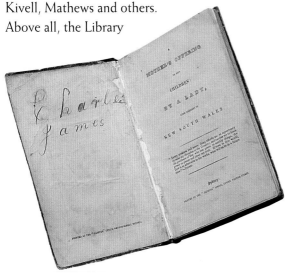

seeks to broaden the scope of these collections by pursuing material from areas neglected in the past. For example, ephemeral items, such as handbills, song sheets, playbills, and the like, all play a part in recording the lives and aspirations of the Australians of yesterday and today. Perhaps even more importantly, books, games and textbooks for children are now very actively sought out. Significant recent acquisitions by the Library include, for instance, two of the earliest children's books set in Australia. In this way, the Library's collections play a dynamic role in Australia's cultural life, responding to the changing emphases and priorities in the quest to preserve our heritage.

A hand-coloured lithograph of H.M. *Warspite* at anchor near Fort Dennison (also known as Pinchgut) in Sydney Harbour, by Augustus Earle, c.1825

A child has lightly coloured the frontispiece and title page of this copy of *A Mother's Offering*, the first children's book published in Australia

23

SOURCES FOR AUSTRALIAN STUDIES: SOME MANUSCRIPT TREASURES

Graeme Powell

*I*n August 1901, a few months after it was established, the Commonwealth Parliamentary Library was offered the records of the Australasian Federation League of New South Wales. Edward Dowling, who had been secretary of the League, told Prime Minister Edmund Barton, that the material in his possession comprised 'printed pamphlets, correspondence and ms. records of the Federation movement in Australia during the past ten years'. He believed that 'this large collection ... would be of great service to Federal legislators and historians'. Several years were to elapse before the Library actually acquired from Dowling the records of the Australasian Federation League. Nevertheless, from the very beginning there was a general assumption that the Library would collect manuscripts as well as books and that its collecting should serve not only the immediate needs of federal parliamentarians but also the future needs of historians and other researchers.

For a long time the collecting of manuscripts was sporadic and largely passive. It was not until the 1930s that staff began to take the initiative by urging parliamentarians and a few other notable Australians to place their papers in the Library. Harold White, who became Librarian in 1947, devoted much time to the pursuit of papers and achieved a great deal of success. By the 1960s the Manuscript collection was comparable in size and significance with that of the Mitchell Library in Sydney, and was far larger than that of any other Australian library. Increasingly, the Library sought not only a wide range of personal papers but also the archives of various national organisations. This dual approach to collecting has continued up to the present time. By 1993 the Manuscript collection occupied about 9000 metres of shelving and comprised several million documents; there were about 1500 substantial collections that had been assembled by individuals and families, and about 300 archives of organisations.

Size by itself is of no significance, for nothing is more common than manuscripts. Every day wastepaper baskets and garbage trucks throughout the country are filling up with papers, many of which contain unique information. Knowing that unique material is constantly being destroyed, collectors face the challenge of identifying and locating the small quantity that might be preserved, taking into account the considerable costs of processing and storing records. The task of the National Library is to preserve private records of national significance, leaving it to the Australian Archives to look after the public records. The significance derives largely from the information contained in the documents: they are preserved because they reveal something of the thoughts, ideas and motives of powerful or influential or creative people, their relationships with other individuals, and the processes whereby they took decisions,

Sunday 29th In the PM Winds southerly clear weather with which we stood into the bay and Anchord under the South shore about 2 Mile within the entrence in 6 fathome water the south point bearing SE and the north point East, Saw as we came in on both points of the bay several of the natives and a few hutts, Men Women and children on the south shore abreast of the ship to which place I went in the boats in hopes of speaking with them accompaned by Mr Banks Dr Solandr and Tupia as we approached the shore they all made off except two men who seem'd resolved to oppose our landing as soon as I saw this I orderd the boats to lay upon their oars in order to speake to them but this was to little purpose for neither us nor Tupia could understand one word they said. We then threw them some nails beeds &ca ashore which they took up and seem'd not ill pleased in so much that I thout that they beckon'd to us to come ashore but in this we were mistaken for as soon as we put the boat in they again came to oppose us upon which I fired a musquet between the two which had no other effect than to make them retire back where bundles of their darts lay and one of them took up a stone and threw at us which caused my foiring a second musquet load with small shott and altho some of the shott struck the man yet it had no other effect than make him lay hold of a target to defend himself immediatly after this we landed which we had no sooner done then they threw'd two darts at us this obliged me to fire a third shott soon after which they both made off but not in such hast but what we might have taken one, but Mr Banks carried out their various activities, or produced books and other works of art. To a lesser degree, the significance derives from either the association of documents with a notable figure or simply their aesthetic or other qualities as artefacts.

The Library has always taken the view that it should collect significant manuscripts from the whole period of European settlement of Australia and not just recent times. It began collecting, however, well into the twentieth century and it has not been easy to locate important papers from the colonial period still in private possession. As the bicentennial Australian Historic Records Search revealed, Australian families and organisations seldom retain records, with the possible exception of photographs, for more than two or three generations. Moreover, many of the early records that have survived are not held in Australia. The Australian Joint Copying Project was set up in 1945 to deal precisely with this problem and in its long history produced nearly 10 000 microfilm reels of manuscripts of Australian and Pacific interest held in Britain. Most of the early manuscripts in the Library were also imported from Britain, either by the Library itself or by private collectors who later transferred their collections to the Library.

The earliest collector associated with the Library was E.A. Petherick. In his years in London he bought, usually for modest prices, a variety of historical and literary manuscripts. He was one of many collectors who took advantage of the unfortunate breakup of the papers of Sir Joseph Banks by Lord Brabourne in 1885. While the main group of Australian papers were purchased by the New South Wales government, Petherick succeeded in acquiring a number of letters and papers written by Banks. They include several drafts, ranging in tone from the sarcastic to the diplomatic, of petitions sent to the Viceroy of Brazil in November 1768 when HMS *Endeavour* called at Rio de Janeiro *en route* to the Pacific. Petherick also obtained a number of letters written to Banks by some of the early officials in New South Wales, such as Arthur Phillip, Philip Gidley King and David Collins, reflecting Banks' role as the patron of the colony in its first thirty years. The Banks manuscripts were received by the Library with the rest of the Petherick collection in 1911.

The lawyer and bibliographer Sir John Ferguson was another great collector associated with the Library. Ferguson lived in Sydney and relied on agents in London to secure many of his books and manuscripts. In 1921 he bought the journal kept by James Burney during part of Cook's second voyage in the Pacific in 1772–73. It is a slight work, consisting of thirty-five folios, written for Burney's family and friends and dealing principally with his encounters with the Maoris, Society Islanders and Tongans. He was the son of Dr Charles Burney, the historian of music, and the journal is unusual in setting out New Zealand and Tongan tunes in musical notation. The journal also contains a chart of the eastern coast of Van Diemen's Land, which HMS *Adventure* explored in March 1773. The Burney journal was acquired by the Library shortly after Ferguson's death in 1969.[1]

In 1923 there was speculation that Ferguson might try to obtain a journal written by Cook himself, which was to be sold by Sotheby's in

London. Covering Cook's first voyage to the Pacific, the journal had been in the possession of his widow and then the Bolckow family of Yorkshire for well over a century. The Public Library of New South Wales was certainly anxious to secure it and the Librarian, W.H. Ifould, was sent to London to attend the auction. The Commonwealth Parliamentary Library stood back at first, but then took the initiative and persuaded the new Prime Minister, S.M. Bruce, to seek the journal for the Commonwealth. The unfortunate Ifould arrived in London only to learn that he was to bid on behalf of the Commonwealth, not New South Wales. He was successful, the purchase price being £5000. The most celebrated item in the Library's collections, Cook's *Endeavour* journal is the quintessential national treasure. It is a substantial volume (with a total of 753 pages) written entirely by Cook, generally in a clear hand which presents few problems for modern readers. It was written throughout the voyage and, while Cook often copied passages from the journals of his shipmates, especially Banks, other passages are more like early drafts. For instance, there are many amendments in the entries in April and May 1770, when HMS *Endeavour* was anchored in Botany Bay. Unlike logs, which consist predominantly of nautical details, the journal is a fascinating narrative of one of the great voyages of exploration, in which the entire eastern coast of Australia was charted, many of its landmarks named, first encounters with the

Australian Aborigines described, and British colonisation of the country was foreshadowed.

Other manuscripts relating to maritime exploration and the first settlement in New South Wales have been acquired at infrequent intervals, generally in London. In 1930 the Library purchased a journal of John Gore, one of Cook's lieutenants, kept on the voyage of HMS *Dolphin* in 1766–68. It was on this voyage, which immediately preceded Cook's first voyage, that Tahiti was discovered. The Library has very little manuscript material relating to the First Fleet, but in 1974 it purchased from a dealer the 1787–89 journal of Arthur Bowes Smyth. Smyth was a surgeon on the *Lady Penrhyn*, which transported female convicts to Botany Bay, and his journal describes in detail the voyage, the depravity of the convicts, and the early months of the settlement at Sydney. Norfolk Island was also settled in 1788 and the Library holds the journal that Philip Gidley King kept for years while in command of this lonely outpost. In addition, it has recently purchased King's copy of John Hunter's book *An Historical Journal of the Transactions at Port Jackson and Norfolk Island*, in which King wrote highly critical marginal notes in the passages dealing with Norfolk Island.

While Governors Phillip and King were establishing colonies at Sydney and Norfolk Island, William Bligh was facing the mutineers on HMS *Bounty*. The notebook that he kept in the open launch on the voyage from Tonga to Timor

Arthur Bowes Smyth's *Journal of a Voyage... in the Lady Penrhyn, 1787–1789* in 1789 was sold at Sotheby's in 1976. The fame of the mutiny, at least partly due to Hollywood, led to predictions of a very high price. The Library, however, secured the support of the Prime Minister, Malcolm Fraser, and bought the notebook, together with Bligh's detailed descriptions of Fletcher Christian and the other mutineers. The notebook, which Bligh kept inside his shirt, is small and lacks the detail of the log that is now in the Mitchell Library. Yet, apart from its enormous romantic interest, it contains a surprising amount of navigational data as well as more personal jottings such as 'Miserably wet' and 'People want Bread'.[2]

Bligh's own description of the *Bounty* mutineers

The Library's holdings of nineteenth-century manuscripts are stronger than many researchers realise. Any unevenness or weakness in parts of the collection result from two factors. Firstly, by the time that the Library became an active collector, outstanding early family collections had mostly been dispersed. Consequently, nineteenth-century manuscripts have usually been acquired from private collectors, such as Ferguson, or from dealers and auctioneers. Secondly, it was only in the last decade or so of the nineteenth century that individuals and organisations of definite national standing began to emerge. Most personal or organisational records of the colonial period relate exclusively or predominantly to a particular town, district or colony and the criterion of national significance is difficult to apply—in these cases the Library has frequently stood aside to allow state libraries to pursue interesting papers relating to their localities.

Private collectors were not so sensitive to the problems arising from the federal system. Rex Nan Kivell assembled manuscripts relating to the early history of all the Australian colonies, as well as New Zealand. In 1958, for instance, he outbid the Mitchell Library for a major collection of papers of Governor Brisbane. Apart from correspondence, the collection contains the original report by John Oxley on his expedition to Moreton Bay in 1823 to select a site for a convict settlement and a petition, written on vellum, calling for 'Trial by Jury, Taxation by Representation and an Elective

Assembly'. There is also a manuscript written in 1825 by the missionary L.E. Threlkeld on the language of the Aborigines of the Newcastle district. John Ferguson collected many manuscripts relating to New South Wales and Victoria in the nineteenth century. His collection is particularly rich in Presbyterian and Wesleyan records and includes a substantial group of papers of John Dunmore Lang. Among the papers of one of the pioneers of Melbourne, John Pascoe Fawkner, acquired by Ferguson was the journal describing Fawkner's expedition from Van Diemen's Land to Port Phillip in 1835 and the stores book for his ship *Enterprise*. The Library also holds two issues of the *Melbourne Advertiser* which Fawkner produced in manuscript form in 1838.

Occasionally there are early manuscripts that transcend colonial boundaries. An outstanding example are the papers of the formidable Lady Franklin, the wife of Sir John Franklin, the Governor of Van Diemen's Land. Her 1839 diary, written in a minute hand, records the first journey overland from Melbourne to Sydney made by a woman. The diary and also the letters to her husband describe in considerable detail the country beyond the frontiers of settlement and encounters with other travellers and settlers, as well as her impressions of Sydney society and her subsequent travels to the Illawarra. Another diary describes a voyage to Adelaide and Kangaroo Island in 1840–41.

As well as travels within Australia, the journeys of immigrants sailing to Australia are well represented in the Library's collections. The writing of diaries, letter-diaries and manuscript newspapers was a feature of shipboard life,

especially in the mid-nineteenth century. They vary greatly in length and interest: some are a litany of winds and monotony, others record disputes and flirtations, while others deal with religion and meditations on the dramatic change in the immigrant's life. Most end, rather frustratingly, with the sighting of land, but a few contain early impressions and experiences of Australian life. Ships' officers also kept journals, often of a superior kind. John Norcock, a mate on HMS *Rattlesnake* in 1835–37, wrote of his detestation of his captain, William Hobson, meetings with Sir Richard Bourke and William Lonsdale, the charting of Port Phillip Bay, and the endless waiting for news from England. Three journals are held of Alexander Weynton, describing nine voyages of merchant ships to

A watercolour sketch from volume 1 of Captain Alexander Weynton's journals, showing the rescue of a balloonist from the shark-infested waters of the Madras roads, 1851

Australia between 1847 and 1860. There are again long passages on the routines of shipboard life, but these are interspersed with lively accounts of the behaviour of passengers and of social events in Sydney and Melbourne. After attending a ball in Sydney he wrote:

I must certainly say that several of the girls are exceedingly pretty but they had large feet and have that peculiar lack of animation which distinguish all Australian women. They danced violently but not well.

The Weynton journals are also exceptional for their detailed watercolours of ships, people and incidents.

Private collections acquired by the Library have sometimes included political papers, such as family letters of Stuart Donaldson (the first Premier of New South Wales) and James Watson (a New South Wales politician) and Thomas Murray-Prior (the first Postmaster-General of Queensland). However, the Library's holdings of political papers essentially date from the Federation movement of the 1890s. The records of the Australasian Federation League were the first major manuscript collection acquired by the Library. In 1928 the first instalment of the papers of Sir Edmund Barton were received from his family and they were followed a few years later by the extensive papers of Sir Littleton Groom. Gradually, both large and small collections were acquired of papers of several of the Federation Fathers and other federal ministers, parliamentarians and officials. By 1993 there were about one hundred such collections. While they vary greatly in interest, as a group they are the most heavily used of the manuscript collections for they document an enormous range of subjects, events and movements in the last century.

By virtue of their occupation, all politicians receive papers. The early politicians had little secretarial assistance, so they wrote most of their own letters by hand. They did not, however, necessarily keep many papers. Thus the papers of Barton occupy only a few boxes and it is evident that most of his correspondence has been lost. Nevertheless, the papers contain some very good material on the Federation movement, including a series of annotated drafts of the Australian Constitution. In contrast, the papers of his friend and successor, Alfred Deakin, are the finest example of a personal collection of an Australian politician. For over thirty years Deakin maintained a huge correspondence with his family and politicians, officials and writers in different parts of the world. Throughout this time he was a Victorian and federal politician and accumulated papers relating to his ministerial and political activities. He was also a journalist for many years. Somehow he found time to read extensively and record in numerous diaries, notebooks and manuscripts his reflections on history, politics, philosophy, theology, psychology and literature. After his death in 1919 the papers passed to his eldest daughter, Ivy Brookes, who presented them to the Library in 1965. In documenting so fully the public career and the private thoughts of an extraordinary man, the Deakin Papers are one of the great treasures of the National Library.

The papers of people in public life are often large and often uneven. William Morris Hughes, prime minister from 1915 to 1923, kept very little relating to his early political and trade union career, which is disappointing to historians studying the origins of the Australian Labor Party. However, his papers contain a good deal on the First World War and as he grew older he seems to have discarded fewer and fewer papers. Similarly, the papers of Sir Frederic Eggleston date almost entirely from the second half of his life, but for that period they are a good record of his political, diplomatic, academic and intellectual interests. In contrast, his friend Sir John Latham retained papers from his schooldays in the 1890s until his death in 1964. Latham did not have the literary and philosophical interests of Deakin, but his career took in law, politics, journalism and diplomacy, and he had a long association with the University of Melbourne and held office in countless organisations. He was a cold, aloof man whose letters seldom sparkled, yet the letters that he received and filed away shed light on many of the major political events and conflicts from the time of Deakin to the last years of the Menzies regime.

The papers of Sir Robert Menzies constitute the largest collection of personal papers in the Manuscript collection. Like Latham, he was not an imaginative letter-writer and it appears that many of his letters were in fact written by his secretary. Yet in his long political career he received letters from many parts of the world, some of which were written with flair and provide personal insights on Australian and international events. Menzies did not consistently keep a diary, unlike his colleague and rival R.G. Casey, but he

did resort to a diary when travelling overseas. These diaries are an excellent record of his impressions of British and European politics and political leaders, particularly the diary he kept of a wartime trip to England in 1941.[3] Menzies was probably the last prime minister to maintain a collection of personal papers. Since the Second World War political collections have grown much larger, but the bulk of the papers have been written not by politicians but by their aides and advisers, and are official rather than personal in tone. Diaries are still sometimes kept, but the rich private correspondence of Deakin or Latham is largely a thing of the past.

As well as parliamentarians, a number of governors-general are represented in the collection. Lord Tennyson was Governor of South Australia as well as Governor-General and his papers span Federation, the Boer War and the early years of the Commonwealth government. Of particular interest are the long series of letters written by Lady Tennyson to her mother in England, describing her travels and high society in the Australian colonies. The papers of Sir Ronald Munro-Ferguson, later Lord Novar, are somewhat less personal, but record the problems and strains

Robert Helpmann as Shylock in *The Merchant of Venice*. He shared star billing in the play's Australian season with the American actress Katherine Hepburn

31

The writer Katharine Susannah Prichard at the time when she was a journalist with the Melbourne *Herald* 1910–11

books and other published writings were originally conceived and subsequently evolved. One of the earliest literary manuscripts acquired by the Library was the draft of Anthony Trollope's book *Australia*, first published in 1873. Trollope was a prolific writer and it is significant that the differences between the draft and the published work are quite minor. In contrast, the novelist Henry Handel Richardson rewrote extensively and her handwritten and typescript drafts reflect her painstaking writing methods. Similarly, the family papers that she collected and her research notes on Australian history provide a great deal of background information on her finest work, *The Fortunes of Richard Mahony*. The poet Kenneth Slessor and the playwright David Williamson are

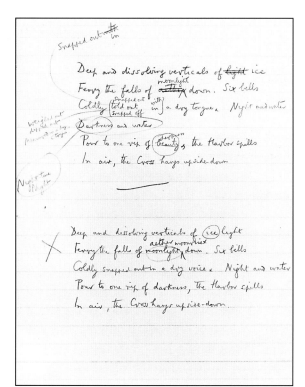

Part of a draft of Kenneth Slessor's poem 'Five Bells'. Note that six bells became five in the final manuscript

in Australia's relations with Britain throughout the First World War. They are a particularly good source on W.M. Hughes and the conscription crises of 1916–17.

The Library has very strong holdings of literary papers, ranging in time from Henry Kendall and Rolf Boldrewood to writers who have emerged quite recently, such as Tim Winton, Marion Halligan and John Tranter. Good literary collections contain not only personal correspondence and papers of the writers, but also drafts and notebooks which document how their other writers whose notebooks illustrate the struggle for the right word. In one of Slessor's notebooks, for example, variations of two lines that appear in 'Five Bells' extend over seventeen pages.

The initial instalment of Henry Handel Richardson's papers, received in 1946, consisted largely of drafts. Over the next forty years more instalments of letters, diaries and other personal papers recording her day-to-day activities and interests were received. Documentation on other writers has also often been assembled gradually over a long time. For instance, letters of Christina Stead have been obtained from many sources and they greatly strengthen the collection that Stead bequeathed to the Library. Patrick White had no interest in placing his papers in a library, although the draft of his last novel, *Memoirs of Many in One*, was bought (jointly with the State Library of New South Wales) after his death. Nevertheless, his friends often retained his letters and several hundred of them have been transferred to the Library, dating from his young days as a jackeroo in the Monaro until 1989.

Of the many literary collections acquired by the Library in the last fifty years, the most comprehensive is almost certainly the papers of Vance and Nettie Palmer. This collection is strong in drafts of novels, poems, plays, and historical, biographical and critical writings. There are also a wide range of personal documents, including the diaries that Nettie kept between 1921 and 1961. Above all, it is rich in correspondence.

Nettie, in particular, corresponded with an extraordinary number of writers, including Richardson, Louis Esson, Frank Dalby Davison, Hugh McCrae, Bernard O'Dowd, Miles Franklin, Eleanor Dark, Katharine Susannah Prichard and many others. The Palmer Papers are in almost constant use by literary historians, while others have drawn on the volume of selected letters published by the Library in 1977.[4]

While the other arts are not as well documented in the Manuscript collection, a number of musicians, dancers, actors and artists have placed their personal papers in the Library. In 1956 it acquired its first music manuscript, the highly illustrated score of *Corroboree*, the ballet suite by John Antill. Following Antill's death in 1987, the remainder of his scores and personal papers were purchased. A fine written and pictorial record of the remarkable career of Sir Robert Helpmann as an actor, dancer and choreographer is contained in a series of albums which he maintained from 1933 to 1982. Most spectacular of all are the diaries and manuscripts of the painter Donald Friend. The diaries were kept continuously from 1942 to 1988 and, as well

An illustrated description of the cast of characters from John Antill's ballet *Corroboree*.

33

as letters and photographs, they contain a huge number of watercolours and pen and ink sketches. The visual splendour is matched by the detailed and often scatological text, which gives a lively commentary on Friend's experiences and travels, and the people whom he loved and hated, in many countries.

The holdings of twentieth-century manuscripts are by no means limited to politics, literature and the arts. The National Library is not a subject library, specialising in one area of human activity, but rather it is a general research library. Although constrained in its collecting by the criterion of national standing, the focus is still broad. Papers are held of graziers and business leaders, journalists and feminists, soldiers and sports figures, religious leaders and philosophers, scientists and lawyers, aviators and economists. A few examples must suffice to illustrate the diversity of the collection. The manuscripts of Daisy Bates constitute a huge body of source material on the beliefs and customs of Aboriginal peoples of Western Australia and South Australia. The papers of Sir John Monash, which are especially strong in correspondence and letterbooks, cover not only his achievements as Australia's most famous soldier but also his distinguished civilian career as an engineer and public figure. The albums of Sir Donald Bradman are a comprehensive written and pictorial record of the career of a legendary cricketer. The records of national organisations are equally diverse, ranging from political parties to learned societies. One of the largest is the archives of the Australian Inland Mission, a magnificent source on social conditions in the outback from the 1920s until recent times.

Compared to the collections of many European and Asian libraries and archives, few of the manuscripts held by the National Library are of great antiquity or beauty. They were

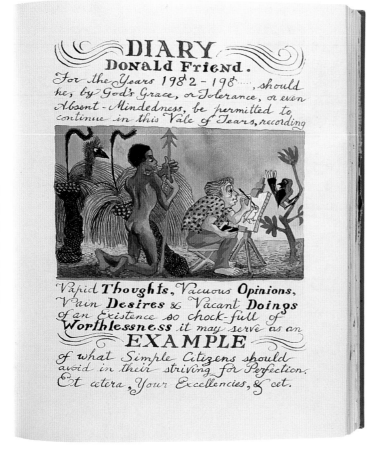

A title page from one of the Library's recent acquisitions, the diaries of the artist Donald Friend

34

Padre David Hurse ministering to stockmen in the Northern Territory: from the photographic record collection of the Australian Inland Mission

mostly written in the last two centuries and, with rare exceptions such as the Weynton journals or the Friend diaries, they have little visual appeal. They do, however, have enormous association interest: the great majority of the collections have a direct link with famous men and women in Australian history. Above all, they contain valuable evidence, much of it unique, of Australian political, social and cultural history and of the ambitions, attitudes and beliefs of many of the people who have visited or lived in the country since the time of Cook.

AUSTRALIA'S CULTURAL HERITAGE: THE VISUAL RECORD

Sasha Grishin

When Sir Joshua Reynolds wrote his *Discourses* in the mid-eighteenth century, ideas on what constituted high art had largely ceased to be controversial. He wrote:

> It must not, indeed, be forgotten, that there is a nobleness of conception, which goes beyond anything in the mere exhibition even of perfect form; there is an art of animating and dignifying the figures with intellectual grandeur, of impressing the appearance of philosophical wisdom, of heroic virtues.

Reynolds highlighted the features which he felt were characteristic of true art and which transformed it above simply being the display of visually observed forms.

At the time when opinions such as Reynolds' held sway, decisions were made as to what art was considered worthy of a place in public galleries and museums. Visual records that simply preserved an exact likeness of people, their natural and built environment and the significant events which shaped their lives were destined to be kept in public libraries, if at all. Australia's earliest public galleries, such as those in Melbourne (established 1861), Hobart (established 1863), Sydney (established 1874) and Adelaide (established 1879), were to some extent created as an attempt to raise the status of the 'noble fine arts' and to differentiate them from simple social documentation. At the same time as the National Gallery of Victoria was acquiring plaster casts of Ancient Greek and Roman sculpture in Britain, the

Tilba Tilba Collection. Mr. Arthur Bate of Corunna, took this photograph around 1895 at Boxsell House, Tilba Tilba

Melbourne Public Library in 1869 commissioned the local painter and printmaker S.T. Gill, to do a series of forty watercolour drawings of life on the Victorian goldfields which he had witnessed in the 1850s. This demarcation and implied hierarchy in the visual arts was inherited by the present century and is the single most important explanation as to why the National Library of Australia has such a magnificent collection of paintings, prints, drawings, photographs and other visual records, which makes it today the envy of most galleries in Australia.

When all the different mediums are brought together, the Pictorial collection of the Library has well in excess of half a million individual images, making it into one of the richest repositories of Australian visual culture. The main criterion for inclusion in the collection is that an image documents the appearance of the Australian peoples or of their neighbours, or their environment, or records their histories. The idea of an 'objective visual record', so dear to those brought up on Enlightenment ideas, has largely been discredited in the past half-century. Even photography, sometimes described as the most mechanical of all the arts, and about which Eugene Delacroix charmingly noted, 'You see only what is interesting, whereas the instrument puts in everything', is more of a commentary on the photographer's values, than on the scene in front of the camera. The photographer does have to make conscious decisions concerning the subject of the photograph, what to include, from what angle, using what equipment and for what purpose. An analysis of even such seemingly neutral genres as portrait and topographical photography, provides much information about the aesthetic and social values of the photographer. For example, group photographs can

illustrate an implied gender hierarchy, or a topographical photograph can reflect an attitude to land use, where a scene of land clearing may be viewed as the first step along the road to progress and a prosperous farming economy, or as a protest at the wanton destruction of a beautiful natural environment. When images are viewed in considerable numbers, apart from their intended role of recording visual data, they can also be read as an enormously important record of the values, aspirations, fears and superstitions of the society which made them.

Although the National Library of Australia acquires pictorial material for its historical significance rather than its aesthetic appeal, this is

A bird with native vegetation from a sketchbook by Captain John Hunter entitled *Birds and Flowers of New South Wales Drawn on the Spot in 1788, '89 & '90*

not to say that a visual representation which is collected primarily for its historic accuracy, almost by definition must be devoid of artistic beauty. In 1920 the Parliamentary Library Committee purchased Tom Roberts' painting *Bourke Street* (previously exhibited under the title *Allegro con Brio, Bourke Street West*) ostensibly because it was an early view of Melbourne. It shows a street in central Melbourne painted just before the tramlines were introduced into Bourke Street in August 1887. Roberts was careful to preserve the

topographic landmarks, from the booksellers Dunn and Collins in the foreground, to P. Philipson & Co. the jewellers and John Danks the gasfitter, right through to the Menzies Hotel at the top of the hill. The painting is also a comment on costume, with two young ladies shown crossing the street in the foreground and decked out in the latest fashion of the day, possibly added by the artist a few years after he finished the rest of the painting. Roberts has incorporated all of these elements to make a

general artistic statement. It is characterised in terms of a sketchy painting technique, a light colour palette and a certain randomness in the compositional structure exploiting small patches of colour which lack clear articulation. Much of this reflects his experiences in England where he increasingly became aware of such painters as J.M. Whistler and Jean Léon Gérôme.

Twenty years earlier, S.T. Gill tackled a view of Bourke Street, this time from the intersection with Queens Street, with the Australia Hotel and Bears Horse Bazaar on the corner. Gill probably drew the scene early in 1856 and it was engraved the following year after he had left for Sydney.

What has changed between the two representations is not so much the appearance of the town, but the artistic conventions employed to depict it. Gill has used a fairly tight perspective with a single vanishing point near the centre of the picture, with the town now becoming a backdrop used to focus attention on the scenes of human interest in the foreground, like the pie-seller and the men arguing. Historians of the city of Melbourne find Gill's documentation important, for example he proves that Lilburner and Anslow horse auctioneers were operating by 1856 at 67 Bourke Street, but he also makes an artistic statement which informs us what was on

Augustus Earle. *View from the Summit of Mount York, Looking Towards Bathurst Plains,... N.S.W,* c.1826

the colonial art agenda at this time, in the same way as Roberts illustrates the values and attitudes which were in vogue a couple of decades later. The changes which these two works illustrate are both to the physical appearance of the place, as well as to attitudes to art and cultural values. The Roberts painting, together with thirty-one other paintings, in recognition of their exceptional value as art objects, while remaining in the collection of the National Library of Australia, have been made available on long-term loan for display at the National Gallery of Australia.

From the origins of the National Library in 1901 it was recognised that the visual record was an integral part of the national cultural archive which was to be systematically assembled by the Library. Pictures entered the collection from a multitude of sources, usually through purchase or bequest. The most famous and the richest single component of the pictorial holdings, is the Rex Nan Kivell collection. Nan Kivell was a connoisseur with a love for history and collecting,

although his passion for comprehensiveness was not matched by attention to scholarly museum practice—a result of which is that much of his vast collection lacks a provenance prior to his acquisition. Nevertheless, it is an immensely important collection with over 1600 paintings and drawings, more than 3000 prints, numerous albums of drawings, photographs and sketchbooks, as well as various art objects such as commemorative marble plaques and carved and painted emu eggs.

As a director of the Redfern Gallery in London, which handled a lot of contemporary, unconventional and innovatory art, Nan Kivell was not locked into many of the aesthetic prejudices of his time. He combined the desire for comprehensiveness of a modern social historian, with the traditional preoccupations of an art connoisseur with fine quality and the hunt for the rare object, such as his thirty-year quest to obtain a painting which he ascribed to Louis Auguste de Sainson. The encyclopedic scope of his interests makes his collection an invaluable research tool which can be approached from many different directions. His main interest could be described as exploring and documenting the various European ventures into Australia, New Zealand and the Pacific in the seventeenth, eighteenth and nineteenth centuries, and along the way he collected such rare treasures as the sketchbook of Captain John Hunter, the glowing Romantic gem-like watercolour paintings of Conrad Martens and the wonderful studies of rural and urban life in early Australia as preserved in the paintings of artists such as Eugene von Guérard, Augustus Earle and Nicholas Chevalier.

Conrad Martens. *Sydney from the North Shore,* [184–]

While the Nan Kivell collection may be the most famous and spectacular single part of the holdings, other major collections, such as the Petherick and the Ferguson, have also added considerably to the number of watercolour paintings, drawings, sketches, prints and photographs, and have provided a depth and comprehensiveness. For example, when the Petherick collection was acquired in 1911, it contained forty-five works by the important colonial artist John Skinner Prout. These collections, when added together, not only provide an incredibly rich and diverse fabric of visual material, but also in many areas, for example nineteenth-century Australian watercolours, provide an unmatched strength. It is this layering of collections, supplemented with careful purchases, which gives this section of the Library its unique character. A researcher into Australian plants and birds will discover the original watercolours of John and Elizabeth Gould (part of the ornithologist Gregory M. Mathews' collection which was presented to the Library in 1939), also the watercolour drawings by John Lewin and Joseph Lycett, and subsequent studies

by Neville Cayley, Adam Forster, E.E. Gostelow and William Cooper, together with about a thousand drawings of wildflowers and birds by Marian Ellis Rowan (purchased by the Commonwealth in 1923.) When material is available in such quantity, not only does it become a reference on the appearance of species, some of which may no longer be extant, but it enables research into questions such as why certain things were depicted and recorded in this manner, and what this may tell us about the society which was commissioning this sort of work.

John Skinner Prout. *Broulee, N.S.W.,* [1843]

Portraiture has always occupied a central place in the Pictorial collection. While today we tend to look at portraits with an almost voyeuristic curiosity hoping to catch a glimpse of the face and the mind of a politician, a crook or of both, one of the traditional ways of thinking about portraiture was that it preserved the features of noble heroes on whom we could model ourselves. This was one of the reasons why the National Library collected and commissioned portraits of governors, statesmen and women, church leaders, judges, sports personalities, and the distinguished men and women of letters and the arts. Beyond satisfying idle curiosity, they provided examples which society could follow. Fortunately the collection quickly outstripped the intentions of the early founders and the drawn, painted and photographed portraits record most facets of Australian life. For example, early daguerreotypes and ambrotypes inform us about details of dress of the people who posed for their portraits, while other early photographs show exact details of the appearance of goldminers. Augustus Earle's *Bungaree, a Native Chief of New South Wales*, 1830,

goes beyond being a portrait of a particular individual; it is also a powerful social document concerning human degradation. While Noel Counihan's *Portrait of Vance Palmer*, 1953, is a brilliant characterisation of one of Australia's finest writers by one of Australia's finest painters. The collection in fact constitutes a de-facto national portrait gallery, but not only of the famous and infamous, but also of all Australians.

Photographs form the lion's share of the Library's pictorial holdings, with thousands of photographs of people, events and of the environment. It is a collection with considerable depth which explores the whole history of photography in this country. Not only are there examples of early daguerreotypes, ambrotypes, tintypes, albumen prints, bromides, autochromes and

Augustus Earle. *Bungaree, a Native Chief of New South Wales*, 1830

42

Danila Vasilieff.
Portrait of Basil Burdett, [c.1930]

Noel Counihan.
Portrait of Vance Palmer, 1953

Adelaide Perry.
Portrait of Dame Mary Gilmore, 1928

stereographs, but also some of the equipment used to make them, including the photographer Harold Cazneaux's first camera. Special collections of photographs have formed around the work of significant photographers. These include an extensive collection of prints and negatives by Harold Cazneaux, and a huge archive of Frank Hurley's prints and negatives, including his work with the Australian troops in France in the First World War and Shackleton's expedition to the Antarctic. Smaller collections have been assembled of photographs by Max Dupain, David Moore, Axel Poignant and Athol Shmith. There are also a number of specialised collections of photographs which focus on a particular theme, such as the E.M. Humphrey

Frank Hurley. The *Endurance* with an iceberg bearing on it during the Shackleton Expedition of 1914–16. The ship was later crushed in the pack-ice

collection, donated in 1962, with over a thousand photographs of ships, harbours, wharves and lighthouses, and the photographs by Herbert Ponting of Captain Scott's expedition of 1910–13 to the Antarctic. As with the paintings, prints and drawings, photographs were first collected as documentation made by the mechanical eye. As the understanding of photography broadened, photographs have become increasingly admired for their artistic qualities, and examples of the work of such photographers as Cazneaux, Dupain

and Moore are widely regarded as outstanding works of art in their own right.

The Pictorial collection is not a static collection, a locked up body of visual data to be plundered only by academic researchers, but it is a collection which has a very active interface with the public. While members of the public are entitled to literally walk off the street and ask to see any part of the national visual cultural heritage, most become aware of the collection through less direct sources. Descriptions of most

Harold Cazneaux.
*Knock-off Time,
Newcastle,* [193-]

of the paintings, drawings and many of the
original prints are available nationally on the
Australian Bibliographic Network database, and
images of 12 000 items are available on videodisc.
There are also numerous books and facsimiles
published by the Library, and individual works or
whole series of works are included in scores of
exhibitions in Australia and abroad. Perhaps most
significantly, collections of visual material,
through the way in which they are organised, also
shape the way we see our past and project our
future. The depth and comprehensiveness of the
Library's Pictorial collection enables anyone
working on any aspect of Australian history and
culture, to also view it within a non-verbal
context. It is this non-verbal visual record, which
gives our perception of Australia's cultural
heritage a new depth and dimension.

Rare maps in context

Terry Birtles

Maps can be valued for a variety of reasons. Some acquire great monetary appeal for their rarity as collectors items. Some are important as benchmarks in the history of map design and the application of particular technology. Some are prized for the information they convey about a particular moment or event in history, often as the record of massive investment of human endeavour. Some serve as legal instruments or provide a highly accurate scientific record. No map is value free.

It is the sociopolitical dimension of cartography which provides a review base, because most maps and charts function as devices funded by governments or merchant houses to provide a record for assisting the administration of territory or an estate. The circumstances of map production and distribution lead to 'humanistic' understanding of the role of maps as images of international, national or personal power, with periods of silence and secrecy providing a hidden agenda to the exploration and expansion of global trading, political and missionary empires of early modern Europe.[1] Thus the Freycinet brothers in 1802 chose to ignore contemporary British nomenclature when surveying the St Vincent's Gulf area by applying the descriptions of 'Terre Napoléon' and 'Golfe Josephine' for obvious political reasons.

Our National Library houses over 420 000 Australian and overseas maps and charts, together with an extensive collection of atlases of which more than 400 are rare editions. The strength of the oldest parts of the collection lies in sequential records of an emerging European global view as various facts of Indian and Pacific ocean navigation added new data to be placed in a whole-world framework for interpretation and meaning. Such widening comprehension can be traced through the substantial number of maps and atlases housed in the Rare Map section, especially the remarkable collections assembled by John Ferguson, Rex Nan Kivell, E.A. Petherick and Ronald Vere Tooley. (Tooley's commentary, *The Mapping of Australia and Antarctica*, is an essential reference for consulting most pre-twentieth-century maps of the region.)

Appropriately, the Library has concentrated its interest upon maritime discovery of the coastline of Terra Australis Incognita, a theoretical continent first imagined by classical Greeks 1500 years before it was ever sighted by a European. Revived in 1531 as a gigantic Antarctic postulation by a French cartographer, Oronce Finé, this concept was popularised in Antwerp by Gerardus Mercator who in 1569 devised a new world map projection which for the first time allowed seafarers to plot a constant sailing course as a straight line. Mercator also coined the word 'atlas' for his marketing of book-like assemblages of maps. A year later, his good friend Abraham Ortelius updated the world map in an atlas which

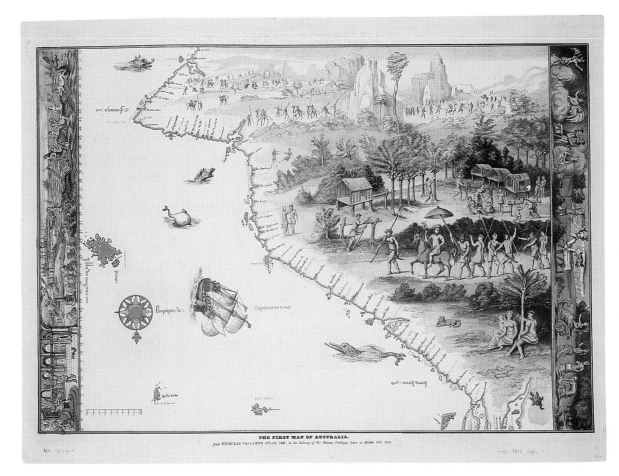

THE FIRST MAP OF AUSTRALIA,
from NICHOLAS VALLARD'S ATLAS, 1547, in the Library of Sir Thomas Phillipps, Bart. at Middle Hill, 1856.

This nineteenth century facsimile of Nicholas Vallard's *First Map of Australia*. was found in 1856 in the library of Sir Thomas Phillipps, Bart.

showed better knowledge of coastline shapes for the *Maris Pacifici* and *Indiae Orientalis*, with Nova Guinea identified as separate from land to the south. The Dutch cartographer Cornelis De Jode, in 1593, added speculation about this mysterious southern continent by populating it with an archer, a snake, a lion and a huge winged lizard or griffin. Was this guesswork, or disguised secret knowledge?

Evidence suggesting earlier Portuguese contact with Australia's shores is now discredited.[2] Facsimiles taken from Nicholas Vallard's atlas of 1547 can be attributed to nineteenth-century propaganda claiming Portuguese discovery. This colourful product, designed to impress financiers, is more a work of art than accurate record, illustrated by European imagination borrowing from classical mythology.

The authenticity of Dutch landings in Australia since 1605 and Spanish knowledge of Torres Strait in that year is clearly testified, although secrecy persisted because of Catholic and Protestant hostilities in Europe. For example, mapping of the west coast of Carpentaria did not

47

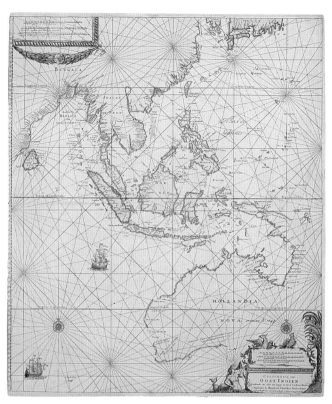

become public until Henricus Hondius designed a revised world map in 1630, with further detail given in the 1633 edition of the East Indies. The Map collection contains some excellent examples of the decorative and artistic Dutch cartography of the seventeenth century.

Two of the rarest items in the collection are sea atlases published by Hendrick Doncker and Sir Robert Dudley. Doncker's *De Zee-Atlas Ofte Water-Waereld* is the only known surviving copy in a public collection of the first edition of 1659. His map of the East Indies illustrates much of Abel Tasman's surveys of the Australian coast (1642–44), but even as a re-engraved form issued in 1696 continued to avoid any indication of the existence of Van Diemen's Land and New Zealand. Dudley's *Arcano del Mare*, published in Florence in 1646, with a second edition in 1661, ranks as the first sea atlas prepared by an Englishman, but it added no new knowledge of New Holland; it even confuses by repeating names in order to fill empty sections of coastline.

Speculation characterises the majority of seventeenth- and eighteenth-century maps by French and Italian geographers who, in the absence of new data, engaged in considerable conjecture about the blank spaces left for unexplored regions. Nicolas Sanson's world map of 1651 repeated outdated suppositions of the previous century for his drawing of Australia's northern coastline. Pierre Du Val in 1686 influenced a succession of map publishers by linking New Zealand to an imagined east Australian coastline. By 1714, French maps had incorporated New Guinea and Terre de Quiros into an uninterrupted continent not redrawn until Robert de Vaugondy showed Torres Strait in 1756—James Cook took this map with him on his first voyage thirteen years later. In Venice, Vincenzo Coronelli artistically filled in the unknown interior of 'Niew Hollandt' with idyllic scenes of native hunters with spears tracking stags or riding an elephant while others lie under the shade of a banyan tree. Excellent examples of Coronelli's work are the engraved facsimile terrestrial globe and celestial globe on display in the Map Reading Room.

The most unusual eighteenth-century product in the Library must be the flight of fancy published in 1754 by Philippe Buache, a prolific writer, who among other ideas attached New Zealand to an Antarctic continent separate from 'Continent Austral'.

It was misinformation of this type which the British government sought to correct once it had established itself as Europe's leading maritime power. The South Sea voyages of Commodore Byron and Captain Mouat (1765), Captains

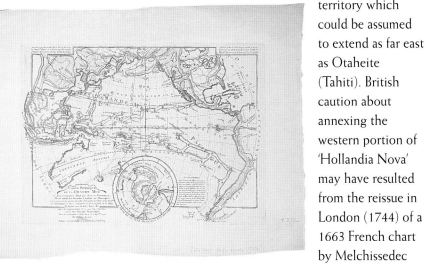

Wallis and Carteret (1767) and Lieutenant James Cook (1769) were funded specifically to extend this knowledge and to gain a better understanding of southern hemisphere astronomy and magnetic variation. William Whitchurch engraved a chart of these voyages which was released for publication in 1773. His uncluttered cartographic style concentrates on mathematical accuracy as an alternative to fiction and represents a new breed of map. For the first time in European history, maps of maritime discovery were issued immediately as public information, with European language copies quickly following.

The British decision to colonise New South Wales represented its developing global maritime hegemony. Governor Phillip's orders were to annexe a larger portion of the earth's surface than ever claimed before, without clear knowledge of whether additional land existed east of New Zealand. It was no coincidence that the first six governors of the new colony were naval officers. Their task was to complete the charting of a territory which could be assumed to extend as far east as Otaheite (Tahiti). British caution about annexing the western portion of 'Hollandia Nova' may have resulted from the reissue in London (1744) of a 1663 French chart by Melchissedec Thevenot, which showed the west coast as a French possession inherited from the Dutch. Emanuel Bowen, publisher of the London edition, inscribed the following words on his map:

> It is impofsible to conceive a Country that promises fairer from its Scituation, than this of Terra Australis; no longer incognita as the Map demonstrates, but the Southern Continent discovered. It lies Precisely in the richest Climates of the World.

On the basis of latitudinal and longitudinal comparison with Sumatra, New Guinea, Africa, Peru and Brazil, Bowen theorised fortunes in precious stones, silver, gold and other valuable commodities to be won by whoever settled there. Together these must have presented powerful incentives for British colonisation of this continent three years later.

The Australian coastline is drawn as conjecture in *Carte Physique de la Grande Mer* by Philippe Buache, 1754

A Complete Map of the Southern Continent Survey'd by Capt. Abel Tasman, 1663 was reissued in London in 1744

The primary focus of the Map collection for the nineteenth century is British Australasia. Generally, the cartography follows imperial designs and standards, but as the years progress there is increasing evidence of the development of local innovations in mapping. Sequences of maps express the frequent changes to administrative boundaries and electoral and police districts. Others function as records of overland exploration, or cover town and village street plans, harbour defences, the location of military posts planned in 1839 between Sydney and Port Phillip, farm subdivisions and squattages, allotment maps and land sale plans. The Ferguson collection is an especially rich source of the latter as records of social history, with some copies traced by hand onto butter paper. Many sale plans feature illustrations of contemporary landscapes and the architecture of particular dwellings and buildings of the time. An example is an 1853 lithograph of Portland in the newly proclaimed colony of Victoria.

Attempts to monitor Crown land alienation in New South Wales influenced land title recording practices in the other colonies. One of the earliest maps to generalise such information, published by William Dymock in 1810, follows an attempt initiated in 1804 to group settlers and convicts in townships of up to 12 000 hectares. By 1820, approximately 130 000 hectares had been granted, but surveyors preoccupied with Admiralty charting, land exploration and surveys had pegged out only 145 farms.[3] Today, local property ownership detail remains the

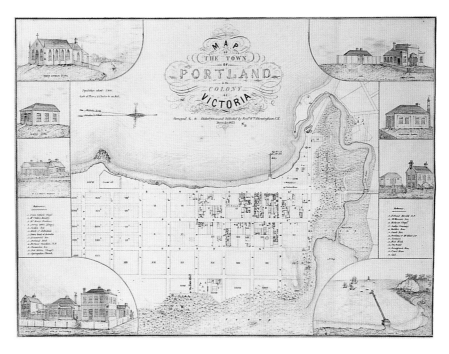

Birmingham's *Map of the Town of Portland in the Colony of Victoria.*

responsibility of state departments, but in the National Library there is no shortage of more generalised maps showing the expansion of settlement during a period of massive European immigration.

One of the most predominant features of colonial maps is the absence of any record of existing Aboriginal settlements. A sketch map by the explorer Lieutenant George Grey RN, of *Supposed Native Tombs Discovered on the N.W. Coast of New Holland* in 1838 is a rare exception. Even where treaties were struck with the original residents, the ethnocentrism of the incoming culture is apparent on cartographic records. For example, an 1865 Stanford map of the province of Auckland in New Zealand categorises land sold, land open for selection by free-grant immigrants

and land 'acquired by the Government from the Natives', with the rest of the map left blank. A map by George Chapman of the same area published in the following year was designed specifically to identify areas of European settlement only. Even by March 1874, the Society for Promoting Christian Knowledge mapped mission stations throughout New Zealand without paying any attention to the structure of Maori tribal organisation. Presumably its British readership simply was not interested.

A British rush for maps of Australasia was triggered by the discoveries of gold and, later, other valuable minerals, almost exactly as Emanuel Bowen had predicted over fifty years earlier. When the exciting news reached London, Edward Lloyd of *Lloyd's Weekly* promptly issued a map of the new *Gold Regions*, with scenes along the road to the diggings sketched around the border. A more formal style of map published in 1851, by James Wyld, geographer to Queen Victoria and Prince Albert, was closely followed by an 1852 Arrowsmith map identifying the goldfields of Turon, Ophir, Louisa Creek, Araluen, Abercrombie River, Mount Alexander and Ballarat. In the same year, the Johnstons in Edinburgh designed a map of the two colonies, with the goldfields listed. John Betts' 1855 'sixpenny map' of the gold regions is similar. All maps were updated frequently and copied by other printers all seeking to keep pace with further gold discoveries.

A New Plan of the Settlements in New South Wales, 1810 is one of the earliest maps to record land titles in the colonies

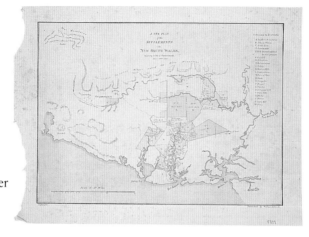

The Gold Regions of Australia... illustrated with scenes along the road to the diggings

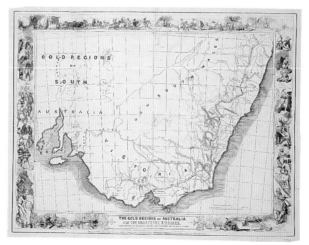

Meanwhile in Australia, a number of local printers produced road guides to the diggings. In Melbourne, Thomas Ham marked out routes to the Victorian diggings as an engraving priced at five shillings. S.T. Leigh of Flinders Lane East issued a cheaper *Digger's Road Guide*, with copies available through Melbourne booksellers and goldfields storekeepers. In Melbourne, Edward Gilks produced an 1858 lithograph, *Emigrants' Guide Map to the Port Curtis Gold Fields. A Road Map and Guide* to the Snowy River district and Kiandra was sold in 1860 by Fergusson and Mitchell of Melbourne.

Subsequent geological maps by each colonial mines department recorded more scientific detail from surface analysis, including maps for the Ballarat and Castlemaine goldfields in Victoria. By 1871, tin and copper districts, together with railway construction, could also be identified on maps of the colonies. One of the finest of these was a *Sketch Map of New South Wales* drawn by J. Tayler, engraved by G.W. Sharp and published in 1876 by the New South Wales Government Printer. An original approach to standardised colour in thematic map design is apparent for a geological and topographical survey of Victoria by Norman Taylor made under direction from the Secretary for Mines. One example is a lithograph of Learmonth by Richard Shepherd.

The rapid progress of colonisation during the latter decades of the century may be judged from the large output of official maps showing railways, roads, mail and electric telegraph routes, agricultural subdivisions and the suburban growth of major cities. Colonial governments also began to issue rainfall maps from observations collected at every post office. Another type of map grew from the needs of tourists using the railways; an *1885 Tourist Map of the Blue Mountains* marks out the bridle track from the railway station to the Jenolan Caves. Private enterprise picked up the responsibility for most atlases and school wall maps; John Sands' *New Atlas of Australia* (published in five volumes in 1886) constitutes the first large scale atlas produced in this country.

The twentieth century has been one of major technological change affecting cartographic practice, largely since the 1930s. Lithographic stones and the teams of map tracers once employed by government and private mapmakers have gradually been replaced by photographic plates and automated digital processes which have reduced the need for manual labour. Data collected remotely by aircraft, satellite or laser beam is assembled by impersonal electronic technology which lacks the artistic qualities of the cartography it has replaced. Increased international standardisation of map design has added new themes such as the distribution and structure of world rainforests or linguistic groupings. With the passage of years, the heritage and professional value of the maps which have continued to be added to the Library's collection have increased in significance.

One 1901 map, *Victoria Classified According to its Productiveness*, effectively marks the high point of handcraftmanship. Released under the directions of that state's Surveyor-General, J.M. Reed, this '16 mile to the inch' map contains a wealth of cartographic information and remains attractive for its simplicity and ease of interpretation. The engraver, James Slight, held an outstanding reputation, together with his father, for their speed and accuracy of workmanship also revealed in the preparation of so many of Victoria's parish maps. The base map continued to be used for other Victorian maps at least to 1959. Coloured overprinting added to each issue of the *Productiveness* map serves as a historic record which in later editions included details such as

Victoria Classified According to its Productiveness 1901 contains a wealth of cartographic information

the location of butter factories and the development of irrigation areas.

Private enterprise has remained vital to Australian cartography, especially the output of H.E.C. Robinson, a Sydney firm responsible for a vast array of wall maps, school and family atlases, street directories, tourist maps and special purpose maps. One of the more innovative Robinson maps is an *Aeroplane View of Sydney* drawn and painted by Sidney Beaumont and D.H. Souter in 1914 when biplane and balloon flights were being made from beaches, racecourses, cricket grounds and isolated fields. A somewhat more sophisticated recognition of the importance of motor vehicles in the reduction of distance for inland families is apparent in *The Inlander* map published in May 1922 by Samuel and Lees of Sydney for the Australian Inland Mission.

The Federation of Australia coincided with a period of nationwide support for British imperialism—from the time of a troublesome Boer War to the conclusion of European hostilities in 1918. British military command maintained an enthusiasm for topographic mapping which infiltrated into Australia. Although the contribution by state mapping services should never be underestimated, the creation of a federal government provided an independent financial base for the emergence of naval, army and national mapping programs. One of the very first Australian maps printed on linen for outdoor use, was designed in 1907 by Lieutenant Colonel W.L. Vernon for field manoeuvres north of Maitland, by the 2nd Brigade of the Australian Light Horse.

Eight years later, ANZAC troops landing at Gallipoli valued the military intelligence assembled for a British 1 : 50 000 *Orographical Map of the Dardanelles* prepared in 1915 in English and French from captured Turkish documents. For the interwar years, Australian topographic mapping remained the responsibility of survey teams of engineers attached to the Australian Section, Imperial General Staff (later Royal Australian Engineers). The Library holds many of the original 'two inch to the mile' plane table surveys drawn between 1911 and 1938. An example for Anglesea illustrates the detail acquired by painstaking field observations.

The threat of Japanese invasion during the early 1940s highlighted the inadequacy of national investment in mapping Australia. Urgent activity by state mapping departments and creation of the Australian Army Survey Corps reflected a new priority towards emergency topographic mapping of a largely unmapped continent. North of Australia a map of the Lutheran mission at Madang, prepared for part of New Guinea by John Mager, ranks as the only topographic map publicly available of that area prior to the outbreak of war. The National Library possesses complete collections of topographic maps by the Corps and its postwar successor, the Division of National Mapping.

Peacetime has now changed the context and focus of Australian cartography. Following completion of a geodetic and topographic base as well as offshore bathymetric surveys, reduced government funding has led to a concentration of resources for digital and statistically-derived maps on such themes as the mapping of census data, environmental information and social indicators. The importance of new types of maps containing

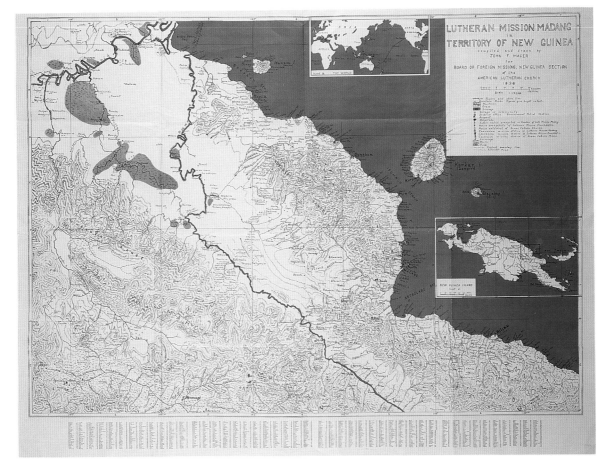

John Mager's
*Lutheran Mission
Madang in Territory
of New Guinea*
1936

social information cannot be underestimated. For example, new maps show the administration of parts of Australia by the Aboriginal and Torres Strait Islander land councils, routes for projected high speed train services and telecommunications networks.

City and non-urban environmental management of the twenty-first century will continue to require an understanding of maps, although the context and the types of data collected may change as the basis of decision making. Maps are acquiring increased use for leisure activity, with multilingual tourist maps for overseas visitors and maps of resorts and national parks gaining wider circulation, together with maps of overseas places Australians feel inclined to visit. The rarity of any map will always remain dependent upon the uniqueness of the message, the design of the product and its cultural meaning. These new forms of maps will in their own way become equally valued treasures.

A JOURNEY TO ASIA

Andrew Gosling

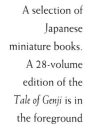

A selection of Japanese miniature books. A 28-volume edition of the *Tale of Genji* is in the foreground

Over the past forty years, the National Library has developed what is now one of the world's leading research collections on Asia. In a sense the development of the collection is a mirror of Australia's involvement with its closest northern neighbours. The starting point was the recognition—not widely accepted in the 1950s—that Australia was closely linked in social and economic terms to Asia and the Pacific region. Since then the Library has collected information on Australia's near neighbours from the point of view of trade and international and cultural relations.

Although much of the Asian collection is devoted to the historical past, at the same time the emphasis is on providing current economic, statistical and political information. For the world of business and government, the treasures of the Asian collection lie in contemporary materials— the information contained in technical journals and statistical reports. For historians and scholars, the treasures are found not only in the information, but in the ideas and often the beauty of the older printed material in Asian languages.

The Chinese, Japanese and Korean language materials in the Library's Asian collections are the largest in the southern hemisphere, and compare favourably with those in the major North American libraries. The contemporary Indonesian and Thai books are almost unrivalled outside their countries of origin. The collection also has a strong component of European language works about Asia which includes a number of outstanding privately established libraries on Asian countries or themes.

People who use the Asian materials come from many sections of Australian society, and the collection serves a number of different needs. In the reading room, an academic compares the media's changing portrayal of women in Chinese magazines produced during the Cultural Revolution to those produced in contemporary China; a Buddhist examines ancient writings from the fifteenth century; a Korean student reads last week's newspapers from Seoul; a government policy analyst scans a Japanese economic journal; a political scientist takes notes from the records of Japanese Socialist Party meetings held in the 1950s. For some, the treasure is in rice production figures from Thailand, a journal article on the results of botanical research in Indonesia, or the beauty of Islamic art.

As an indication of the scope and relevance of the Library's Asian collection, this chapter explores some of the connected but contrasting elements which give these holdings their character. These range from Buddhism and its development in Asia, the span of Korean history from the fifteenth century, Portugal's role as the first European power in Asia, to a Western perspective of Japan and contemporary Indonesia. This collection provides Australians with the means to better understand the place of their own country in a region of close geographic proximity and which provides some of this country's most important trading partnerships. At the same time, the collection serves to remind Australians of the complex cultural and historical identity of Asia which is so important to any understanding of this diverse region.

Buddhism, which may be described as the chief cultural link between the peoples of Asia from India to the Pacific, is well represented in the collection. The historical Buddha, known as Sakyamuni, lived around 500 BC in northern India. His teachings spread widely across Asia over a period of centuries, absorbing many other religious beliefs along the way. The Buddhism of China, Japan and Korea, for example, differs considerably from that of Sri Lanka, Burma and Thailand which remains closer to the early teachings.

Around the first century BC Buddhism began to develop a sacred literature, originally written in two related Indo-European languages, Pali and Sanskrit. The Buddhist Scriptures are known as the Tripitaka (meaning literally 'three baskets') consisting of the disciplines for monastic life, the major teachings and scholars' commentaries on the teachings.

In 1987 the Library's Buddhist collections received a major addition through the donation of a unique library. For several years the Liao family and other benefactors had been building up the Australian Buddhist Library housed in Sydney's Chinatown and open to the public. In order to give it a more secure future the collection was donated to the National Library. The move to Canberra involved careful packing of the 3000 books, which included editions of the scriptures in Chinese, English, Pali, Burmese and Thai—and a bronze replica of a twelfth century Thai Buddha weighing 184 kilograms. For the Liao family, the motivation for donating the collection to the Library—rather than to a temple—was that it would be more easily accessible to Buddhist monks and scholars interested in Buddhist philosophy and religion.

The charmingly illustrated *Life of the Minorities in Southwest China* features butterfly bindings between wooden blocks

57

The Khmer language Tripitaka is the rarest edition of the Buddhist Scriptures held by the Library. It is believed to be one of only a handful remaining after the wholesale destruction of books during the Khmer Rouge regime in Cambodia (1975–79). The Library's set had been purchased in 1970 as part of the Coedes collection on Indochina. Professor Georges Coedes was director of l'École Française d'Extrême Orient, and had collected widely during his long career in former French Indochina.

Another rare edition held is the *Koryo Taejang-gyong* (Tripitaka Koreana) in 1340 volumes. The Library has one of only eight copies in the world produced in Korea in the 1960s from wood blocks engraved in the mid-thirteenth century. The original blocks were carved in a vain effort to seek divine intervention against the Mongol invasion of Korea.

Probably the most beautifully produced Buddhist text is the Nyingma edition of the Tibetan Tripitaka. The Library's copy is from a limited edition of 100 numbered copies. This massive edition contains canonical texts as well as colour and blockprint reproductions of many Tibetan Buddhist art works and research aids presenting comparative information from Tibetan, Chinese, Mongolian and Western sources.

The Khmer Tripitaka is a rare item in the Asian collection

The Library's materials relating to Buddhism range over many aspects including its social and political dimensions. From Thailand, an overwhelmingly Buddhist country, the Library has a major set of cremation volumes. These uniquely Thai publications are produced in limited numbers to honour a deceased person, and are distributed at his or her funeral. They contain a short biography, tributes from family and friends, and often extracts from the subject's own writings, a favourite piece of literature, or something concerning a topic which has been of special interest. Cremation volumes are particularly valuable as they often contain information about important people which is not found elsewhere, and for historians they provide a rare and personal insight into the subject's life and times.

The Library has the largest and most actively developing Korean language collection in Australia. These materials have generally been purchased, or obtained through exchange with major libraries in North and South Korea. However, in 1984 the Library received an important gift of old and rare Korean titles. These had belonged to Mrs Jessie McLaren, who went to Korea from Melbourne with her husband, a medical practitioner, in 1911. Her interest in Korean culture led her to collect many books, some of which she was able to bring back to Australia during the Second World War. Following her death, her daughter, Mrs Rachel Human, donated the material to the Library, so that the books could be kept safely and be freely available for use.

The McLaren-Human collection, as it is now known, contains books dating from the fifteenth to the early twentieth centuries, primarily relating to Korean history and literature. The earliest publication *Samgang Haengsilto* (The Three Principles of Basic Human Relationships) is believed to date from 1490. This book consists of traditional Chinese tales about children obedient to their parents and ministers loyal to their rulers as examples of good Confucian behaviour. A particularly interesting feature is that each page contains an illustration flanked by a description in Chinese with the same story reproduced in Korean script above. Some of the stories and illustrations are quite graphic in their depiction of virtuous people maintaining their loyalty even under torture.

In its collecting program, the Library has emphasised the modern history of Asia, concentrating on reactions to imperialism and the emergence of nationalist movements and subsequent governments. For example the Chinese collection, the largest of the Library's Asian language holdings, is strong on mid-nineteenth century and later developments including the overthrow of the Ch'ing (Manchu) dynasty in the 1911 Revolution, the growth of the Nationalist and Communist movements, and of more recent events such as the Cultural Revolution (1966–76) and its aftermath. The growing number of Asian scholars in Australia find that this twentieth-century focus of the collection allows for close study of periods of dramatic social and political change.

But for those with an interest in earlier history, the Library holds many examples of pamphlets and wall posters from the Taiping movement. The Taiping Rebellion (1850–64), one of the greatest upheavals in modern Chinese history, is particularly well represented both in Chinese and Western sources and in contemporary as well as later works.

The Taiping movement was founded by Hung Hsiu-ch'uan, a visionary leader influenced by Protestant missionaries. Hung preached a mixture of Christian egalitarianism and traditional Chinese utopian ideas. He and his followers captured Nanking in 1853 and looked as if they

Two of 124 volumes in the Tibetan Buddhist canon published in the United States by Dharma Press

59

would overthrow the ruling Ch'ing dynasty. However, Chinese forces with some aid from mercenaries led by the American Frederick Townsend Ward and later Major Charles George Gordon of the British army, finally crushed the rebellion. A statue of 'Chinese' Gordon was erected in central Melbourne commemorating his part in these events.

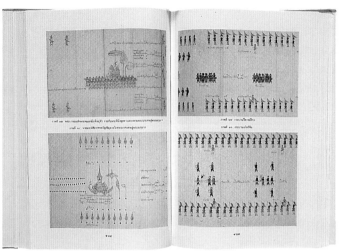

Materials on the Taiping movement in the Asian collection include contemporary items acquired from the London Missionary Society. Of particular significance are twenty-four pamphlets published by the rebels and two original proclamations from the Taiping leaders. Issued at the height of the movement in 1853, the proclamations claimed success for the Taiping armies and urged the people to be peaceful and carry on with their normal lives.

Collecting material from the diverse Asian region depends on maintaining a formal network of libraries and book suppliers, occasionally supplemented with a local presence or visit. A desk-sized box of publications arrives from Japan every few weeks, while Chinese, Indonesian, Thai and Korean shipments arrive regularly, and newspapers and magazines are delivered by air mail each day.

The depth of the Library's Asian collection owes a great deal to the foresight and dedication of individuals who have made their own collected material available to the Library. One benefactor, Jose Maria Braga, created a diverse and outstanding collection which covers Portuguese activity in Asia.

Braga was a businessman, teacher and author based in Macao, who wrote numerous books and articles about this Portuguese settlement. While his collection covers Portuguese influence worldwide its main concentration is on Macao, Hong Kong, China and Japan. The greater part of his library of books, manuscripts, pictures, newspapers and journals was purchased by the National Library in 1966. The collection reminds us that modern European expansion in Asia began with the Portuguese in the late fifteenth century. This small seafaring nation sought trade and Christian converts in competition with the Muslim Arabs who then dominated contact with the Far East. Portugal's role as the first European colonial power in Asia—retaining outposts at Goa, Timor and Macao for four centuries—remains important to an understanding of the Asia of today.

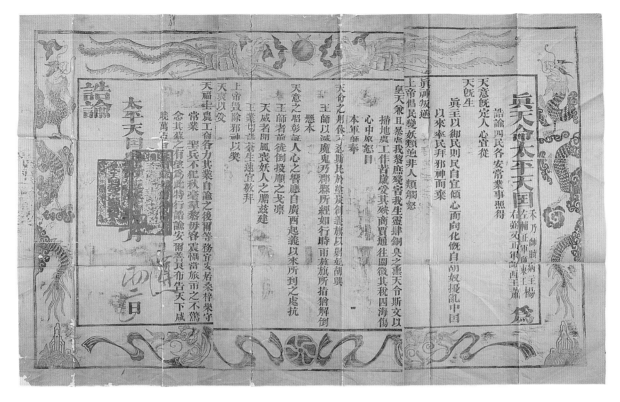

This original wall poster from the Taiping Rebellion, circa 1853, measures 96 x 204 cm

Most of the manuscripts in the Braga collection are copies of documents held in various archives and libraries in Europe. (However, some of these original documents have since been lost.) Manuscripts by Braga himself include his translations and notes relating to the Jesuits in Asia, a handbook of Portuguese officials and their contemporaries in China, and a biographical index to European expansion in East Asia. Other parts of the collection cover topics ranging from Allied and Axis propaganda during the Second World War to the treatment of internees and war crimes trials.

Braga also collected around a thousand pictures relating mainly to his interests in East Asia. These consist of watercolours, prints,

engravings, line drawings and several oil paintings, and the subjects covered include religious and other buildings (especially in Macao), many ships, portraits of missionaries and scenes of traditional life in China and Japan.

While Braga concentrated largely on the activities of one European country in Asia, the Harold S. Williams collection constitutes one of the world's finest resources on Western contact with Japan, in particular the role of foreigners in Japan since its opening to the world in the middle of the nineteenth century.

Harold Williams was born in Victoria in 1889. He studied medicine at the University of Melbourne and at the same time took Japanese language lessons from a Mr Inagaki who ran a local laundry business. In 1919 he visited Japan on holiday to improve his language skills, but deferred his return to Australia after being offered a position with a foreign firm. He was to spend almost his entire adult life in Japan, as a businessman, writer and collector. His extensive library documents the contributions made by Westerners to Japanese life and culture, their role in Japan's modern history, and all aspects of foreign settlement in that country. Not surprisingly, Williams took a particular interest in the subject of Australians in Japan. His collection also includes a large number of pictures and photographs of the foreign communities in Kobe (where Williams and his family lived for many years), Nagasaki and Yokohama.

Williams was also a prolific author. He wrote several books and numerous journal and newspaper articles about Westerners in Japan, including a long-running series entitled 'Shades of the past' in the *Mainichi Daily News*. This began in 1953 and the final article, published posthumously in February 1987, explains his motivation and attitude to careful documentation of the past: 'The need for accurate accounts of the happenings in pre war Japan and especially of the early foreign settlement days had become evident from the amazingly superficial accounts which were then appearing.'

During the late 1960s Williams decided that his collection should be placed in a major library in Australia for safekeeping and to benefit future research. He presented it as a gift to the National Library and established a trust in perpetuity for the development and maintenance of his collection. Through the generosity of his widow,

the National Library has subsequently been able to purchase further English and Japanese language publications to add to the Harold S. Williams collection. Mrs Williams has also donated her own extensive library of Japanese and Chinese art books, and further manuscripts and pictures.

Contemporary Indonesia holds a fascination for Australia on a range of levels, from trade to culture, a reflection in part of geographical proximity. As a reflection of this interest the National Library has developed what is now one of the world's finest modern research collections outside Indonesia itself.

Initial efforts in the 1950s to buy Indonesian publications through booksellers proved largely ineffective. Consequently, the Library opened an office in Jakarta to obtain current books for itself and other Australian libraries on a cooperative basis. This arrangement was formalised in the establishment, in 1971, of the Indonesian Acquisition Office attached to the Australian Embassy in Jakarta. Through this cooperative scheme the Library has collected extensively on Indonesian modern history and social sciences, particularly politics and government, economics, development studies, social issues, statistics and law. Publications collected include not only books but also many capital city and provincial magazines and newspapers. Most of the works are in Indonesian, as well as some regional languages such as Javanese and Balinese.

Staff from the Indonesian Acquisition Office regularly visit book stores, publishers, government offices and universities to purchase or arrange exchanges of books. Regional titles unavailable in the capital have been obtained on acquisition trips

A cloth page from *Samgang Haengsilto* [The Three Principles of Basic Human Relationships]. This Korean manuscript dates from 1490 and is the oldest in the Asian collection

to major provincial centres as far afield as Aceh at the northern tip of Sumatra to Irian Jaya on the eastern half of the island of New Guinea. The Library is continuing to develop its collection through an expanded acquisition and liaison role in Indonesia and Southeast Asia in general.

The Asian collection has been built on a foundation of close cont act with librarians, publishers, educational bodies and other organisations throughout the region. In simple terms, that network of relationships ensures the continued development of a collection which captures the contemporary—not only the past. As Australia further extends its links with countries in the Asia–Pacific region, the National Library's Asian treasures and the collection of which they are so integral a part, will play an increasingly important role for those seeking information about and understanding of this country's northern neighbours. For Australia's own Asian population and for Australians whose ancestry rests in Asia, the collection will serve as an important cultural and heritage resource, a means to assist in the nourishing of roots and the maintenance of a sense of personal identity.

RARE BOOKS:
GEMS IN THE MATRIX

Margaret Dent

There is a kind of rock known to geologists as 'conglomerate', made up of mineral fragments of varying composition and size, all cemented together. The components vary widely and are often water-worn. Substitute 'time' for 'water' and the description fits the National Library's Rare Books collection rather well: a present whole made from many parts of varying origin, a mixture of similarities and differences.

The Rare Books collection has its roots in the Library's earliest beginnings, when some books which were acquired purely for their content were acknowledged as rare or special and therefore in need of extra care. During the Library's early years they were stored in various places of safety, and were only gathered together as a separate collection when the present building was opened in 1968. Since then the Rare Books collection has grown to about 70 000 items, chiefly as a result of the visionary collecting during the 1960s by the then National Librarian, Harold White, and his staff. The collection excludes works in Asian scripts and material which is specifically Australian, as these two categories are covered by other collections elsewhere in the Library. The main strengths of the Rare Books collection are British and European. Given the early history of Australia, this is entirely appropriate, and reflects our origins and the history of exploration and discovery in the Pacific area. It is, therefore, a heritage collection just as the more obviously Australian Ferguson and Nan Kivell collections are: our nation's roots go back beyond 1788, and the Rare Books collection encapsulates much of our earlier heritage. It is strong in a number of subject areas, for example English literature (particularly drama), English linguistics, religion, British social, political and economic history, the French Revolution, and the history of printing. Two country house libraries are included—the Clifford collection from an English noble family, and the de Vesci collection from an Irish one. Among all this there is plenty of scope for the gleam of jewels, some obvious to all, others precious to those seeking an item which may be obscure to many.

The cornerstone of printing in the western world is the Gutenberg *Bible*, also known as the 42-line *Bible*, which is the first book known to

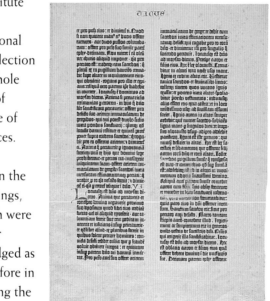

A leaf from the 42-line Gutenberg *Bible* printed in Mainz, Germany around 1455

The rich patina of hand-tooled leather bindings complements the illuminations in this limited facsimile edition of the Gutenberg *Bible*, published in Paterson, NJ, by Pageant Books have been printed in the West from movable type (where the type was set letter by letter and after use could be 'distributed', then re-set to produce other works). Earlier books had been printed from a single carved block, which was naturally faster than manuscript production but was restricted to the one use, and difficult if not impossible to correct if a mistake occurred during its making. Johann Gutenberg developed the technique of printing from movable type in Mainz in the mid-fifteenth century; the 42-line *Bible* was his first known work and was completed in 1455 or 1456. Few libraries are fortunate enough to own a Gutenberg *Bible*; the National Library of Australia has a single leaf (from Leviticus, chapters VI and VII) from this great cultural icon, as well as a beautifully illuminated twentieth-century facsimile of the whole *Bible*.

The sale of single leaves of a precious work is often deplored, and if a perfect or even a good copy were broken up for this purpose, it would be unjustifiable by any ethical standards. The sale of leaves from a badly damaged or very incomplete copy, however, is more acceptable, as such a copy could not be used as a text, and individual leaves at least allow an institution or collector to have a specimen to show as an example of the work.

The earliest complete work in the Rare Books collection is a 1478 edition, published in Venice, of Jacobus de Voragine's *Legenda aurea*—the Golden Legend, or lives of the saints. This was compiled between 1255 and 1266, and circulated in manuscript form for about 200 years; after Gutenberg's development of movable type it was put into printed form for an even wider

audience—the first printed version appeared in 1469. Its popularity is evidenced by the fact that the Library has not only the 1478 version, but a 1486 and a 1496 version; all three came to the Library from different sources.

These incunables (books printed before 1501) are evidence of the durability of early book production techniques—printed with hand-made ink, on paper made from rag stock, and bound by hand in leather over wooden boards. Over 500 years old, and certainly having been well used in their lifetime, they are generally still in excellent condition.

Given the social conditions of the time, religious works were, not surprisingly, heavily represented in the early output of printing, but they were not the only books being produced, and Hartmann Schedel's *Liber cronicarum* (often known as the Nuremberg Chronicle) was a history of the world from a German point of view. The National Library has a copy of the first edition, which was printed in Latin in July 1493. Latin was widely, though not universally, understood at the time, and a German translation of the work appeared in December of that year, entitled *Die Weltchronik*. Both were printed by Anton Koberger, who had begun printing in about 1470 and was an enterprising businessman with a flourishing export trade in his books. The work contains over 1800 woodcut illustrations by Michael Wolgemut and his stepson Wilhelm Playdenwurff. Quite a few of these are handcoloured, and many of them also appear more than once, with the same portrait or view of a town representing widely differing subjects—economical but confusing!

One of Michael Wolgemut's pupils was Albrecht Dürer, who was apprenticed to him from 1486 to 1490. Woodcut illustration is an ancient art, but its practice in Europe was not artistically highly developed before Wolgemut and Dürer. While Wolgemut is today not widely known, Albrecht Dürer's work has achieved world renown and is loved by many. Like Hartmann Schedel, and his master Michael Wolgemut, Dürer came from Nuremberg, and later worked in both Basle and Strasbourg. In 1511 he produced two works on the Passion of Jesus Christ—known as the Large Passion and the Small Passion because of the size of the woodcuts. The Library has a copy of each *Passio christi*, and while both are magnificent, many people find the Small Passion particularly appealing—possibly because, at only 18 cm high, it is on a very personal scale. The Library's copy is very well preserved, and the thirty-six woodcuts in it are, with their flowing lines and deep rich black and clear white, beautiful and very moving.

After its invention in about 1455, printing spread rapidly across Europe, and in due course was brought to England by William Caxton, an English merchant who had learnt the art in Germany—probably in Cologne, where he lived from mid-1471 to late 1472. In 1474 Caxton began printing in Bruges, where he issued, among other works, the first book to be printed anywhere in English, *The Recuyell of the Historyes of Troy*. In 1476 he returned to England, where he printed several small undated items, before producing in 1477 the first dated work printed in England: *The Dictes or sayengis of the philosophres*, translated from French by Anthony Woodville, Earl Rivers, and revised and enlarged by Caxton at Rivers' request.

Most of the works Caxton published were in English, often his own translation, and although the Library has no complete original work of his, it does have a single leaf from his revision of Trevisa's translation of Ranulf Higden's *Polychronicon*, which he printed in 1482. The *Polychronicon* was a universal history written sometime in the 1320s, and widely circulated in manuscript form—about one hundred surviving manuscripts are known.

Caxton's trailblazing career as a printer in England extended over only fourteen years. It was, however, an intensely productive period; and more than one hundred of his works are known, totalling over 18 000 pages. On his death in 1491 Caxton's foreman, Wynkyn de Worde, took over the business, and was even more productive, issuing about eight hundred works altogether: the technology of the craft was improving and the populace was becoming more literate, so the

Albrecht Dürer cut the woodblock for this engraving in 1509 and used it in his book the *Passio christi*, also known as the Small Passion demand for books was growing rapidly. Wynkyn de Worde's output was varied as well as large. He continued to print Caxton's popular translations, but added textbooks, school primers and broadsheets, and began experimenting with non-Roman scripts. The Library's example of his work is a nice combination of Wynkyn de Worde and Caxton, as it is Wynkyn de Worde's 1527 publication of Caxton's translation of the *Legenda aurea* of Jacobus de Voragine. It is not a perfect copy, unfortunately, as quite a few leaves are missing.

The art of printing has ensured the survival of much of our literature which might otherwise have been lost, or so altered during oral or manuscript transmission that the original form and content would have been changed beyond recognition. As it is, there is plenty of scope for discussion of an author's intentions and the relative merits of various editions when scholars analyse early printed works—for example Shakespeare's plays in their Quarto and First Folio editions. The Library's copy of the First Folio *Merchant of Venice* stands serenely apart from the debate. Detached at some stage in the past from the parent volume *Comedies, Histories and Tragedies*, published in 1623, it was beautifully bound earlier this century by the British firm Sangorski and Sutcliffe in red morocco tooled in gold.

The invention of printing not only preserved material from loss or unwarranted alteration, it opened the doors to the spread of intelligent speculation on the human condition, and critical enquiry about the world we live in. John Locke's *An Essay Concerning Humane Understanding* was first published in 1690; the Library has a copy of the fourth edition published in 1700 'with large additions'. In it Locke sets out to analyse human knowledge, its basis in our perceptions, and the concept of the idea. It was a complex task and the topic was one of enduring interest: it is not surprising that the basic questions posed by Locke are still under discussion.

No account of the treasures of the Rare Books collection would be complete without mention of Samuel Johnson's *A Dictionary of the English Language*, which was first published in 1755. In 1974 the Library bought a superb collection of works on English linguistics, which contained a number of early editions of Johnson's *Dictionary*, but, unfortunately, not a first edition. As one of the turning points in the history of the English language, the *Dictionary* was high on the Library's desiderata list; fortunately a copy was acquired in 1979. The importance of the *Dictionary* stems not so much from the undeniably formidable achievement of one man in its compilation, as from the principles upon which it was based: regularised spelling, full and often amusing definitions of words, and quotes from a variety of authoritative sources to illustrate the word definitions. Its success is measured by the number of editions in which it appeared, and in its influence on later dictionaries—notably the *Oxford English Dictionary on Historical Principles* (1884–1928) and Noah Webster's *An American Dictionary of the English Language* (1828).

Only twenty-one years after publication of the benchmark English dictionary, came the benchmark English treatise on economics. Adam Smith's *An Inquiry into the Nature and Causes of the Wealth of Nations* was written over a period of ten years and finally published in 1776. This seminal work traces the history and development of economic theory, and analyses the importance of the labour force in the economy. The work can only be described as a classic, and its high monetary value these days seems rather fitting, considering its subject matter. Also fitting is the source of the Library's first set: a collection of British economic and political history material known after its collector, Leon Kashnor. (A second set came to the Library as part of a donated collection of mostly Australian material.) From the time of its first publication, Smith's *Wealth of Nations* achieved immediate success, and the Library holds many of the subsequent editions.

Outside England, momentous events were occurring. The French Revolution caused an enormous upheaval in Europe, and had far-reaching effects both politically and socially in many countries apart from France. It created a tidal wave of pamphlets, and a group of over 11 000 of these is held by the Library. One of the Revolution's early—and most important—achievements was its declaration of the rights of man, which was adopted by the National Assembly on 26 August 1789. The unassuming appearance of the slim pamphlet entitled *Procès-verbaux de l'Assemblée Nationale Contenant les Articles qúelle a Adoptés de la Déclaration des Droits de l'Homme & du Citoyen* belies its great social significance and its enduring historical importance.

The *Déclaration* consists of an introduction and seventeen brief 'articles'. It was designed to have universal application and is, therefore, one of the great statements of the rights and dignity of humankind. It was swiftly and widely accepted, and received much publicity in the Press, being revised and republished in many forms. When in 1948 the United Nations issued its Declaration of Universal Human Rights, it not only introduced the then new concept of cultural difference, but acknowledged a debt to the original French version of 1789.

Thomas Robert Malthus is best known for his work *An Essay on the Principle of Population* (though as the work is often misinterpreted and misrepresented, 'best' known is perhaps not entirely accurate). The Library has various editions of it, but perhaps even more interesting is the copy of Malthus' *Principles of Political Economy* presented by Malthus himself to the statesman Lord Grenville. This copy is interleaved with 113

Title page from the *Proceedings of the French National Assembly, 1789*, in which the adoption of the Declaration of the Rights of Man is recorded pages of handwritten notes by Grenville commenting on the points of difference between Malthus and the economist David Ricardo, and on the concept of labour as a standard of exchangeable value. This item is absolutely unique, and offers a fascinating and detailed contemporary response to an important work, by a statesman who was closely involved with the issues which formed the work's subject. It is also unusual in that it was never bound in leather but is still as it was issued, in the original boards with a paper label.

Social experiments are often dismal failures, but Robert Owen's work at New Lanark in Scotland was very successful. He improved working and living conditions for the inhabitants of a small mill town and set up schools to educate their children. From being a miserably depressed community, New Lanark became the model for Owen's theory on the importance of early influences in forming character. In 1813, he published *A New View of Society, or, Essays on the Principle of the Formation of the Human Character*. This was very popular, and by 1818 had appeared in four editions, all of which are held by the National Library. Though Owen's theories later fell into disuse, they contained the germ of socialist principles (in fact Owen coined the word 'socialism' around 1835), and the New Lanark experiment is a testament to what can be achieved by the application of commonsense and humanity in society.

Works on animals and natural history have always been popular, as is witnessed by some of the early manuscript bestiaries which described animals both real and fabulous (though the representation of some of the real but little known creatures often leant more to the fabulous). The 44-volume *Histoire Naturelle, Générale et Particulière* compiled by a team supervised by the naturalist Georges Louis Leclerc, comte de Buffon, was first published between 1749 and 1804, and found ample scope in describing the real in nature. It included images of an elephant and a rhinoceros which, though quaint to today's eyes, are certainly recognisable. The work was not restricted to descriptions and images of animal life, but also contained 'a theory of the earth, a general history of man, of the brute creation and of vegetables, minerals, etc'. The time was obviously ripe for such a wide-ranging and scientific approach, and the work was extremely successful; it appeared in many versions and translations. The National Library holds one of these, a translation and adaptation by J.S. Barr which appeared in ten volumes over the years 1797–1807.

As the nineteenth century progressed there were more changes in the methods of book production than there had been in the preceding four centuries. These increased both the numbers and the speed of production of books, but not necessarily their technical quality.

With a lifelong interest in the various manifestations of the arts, and dissatisfied with the quality of books produced commercially at the time, William Morris set up, in London in 1891, the Kelmscott Press to raise the standard of book design and production, revive the personal involvement of the printing and design workers in what they produced, and restore the nexus of art and craft. Kelmscott Press books were often illustrated by Morris's old friend, the artist Edward Burne-Jones. Each work was exquisitely designed, very decorative, superbly printed using the finest materials, and as a result, invariably became a collector's item; the National Library is fortunate in having three items from the press. One particularly interesting example is a volume containing two works: the first, *The Order of Chivalry* translated from the French by William Caxton, edited by F.S. Ellis and printed 'by me William Morris at the Kelmscott Press'. The second in the volume is a French poem entitled *L'Ordene de Chevalerie*, with an English translation by Morris himself. The colophon of the first work is dated 10 November 1892, while the colophon of the second is dated 24 February 1893. They were, however, designed to be published together, as the paging throughout is continuous. The style of the book is typical Kelmscott, with heavy but clean black inking in an ornate typeface and marginal notes printed in red. There is a frontispiece by Burne-Jones and a decorative border by Morris. The whole work recalls Morris' interest in the very early days of printing and in the late medieval world which gave birth to this revolutionary process.

While perhaps not as influential as the development of printing from movable type, the invention of moving pictures and the consequent development of the motion picture industry have nevertheless had a profound effect on society. The early history of the industry, up to 1926, is told in Terry Ramsaye's *A Million and One Nights; a History of the Motion Picture*. The Library's copy is number 98 of an edition limited to 327 copies, all signed by the author and by Thomas Alva Edison, inventor in the late 1880s of the technological foundation of the art of the motion picture: the motion picture film and camera, and the Kinetoscope or peep-show machine which was the ancestor of the projector. These signatures alone would make the book a historic document, but the work is also signed by a galaxy of motion picture identities,

Volume 1 of Terry Ramsaye's *A Million and One Nights; a History of the Motion Picture* is signed by a galaxy of motion picture identities, among them Cecil B. de Mille and Mary Pickford including Mary Pickford, Cecil B. de Mille, D.W. Griffiths, Charles H. Christie, Adolph Zukor, James L. Lasky, Samuel Goldwyn, Earl E. Shauer and David Frohman.

Although a large proportion of the National Library's Rare Books collection was printed before 1801, not all rare books are old, or even elderly. An important part of the collection is modern typographical material, documenting and illustrating developments in the production of high-quality books. An example of this is *Matrix: a Review for Printers and Bibliophiles*, an annual periodical published by the Whittington Press in England. It is a limited edition, on fine paper, which contains both authoritative articles (by contributors expert in their fields connected with book production) and a wealth of illustrative material such as plates, photographs, paper samples, text samples and type specimens. The size of the edition is limited by the availability of the samples—one reason for a genuine limited edition, which is in contrast to an artificially limited edition where the only reason for the limitation is an attempt to increase demand for the work. Another genuine reason is evident in a work containing illustrations printed from plates, where the plates would wear and the quality would suffer if too many copies were printed. A case in point is the selection from Aesop, *Four Fables*, by Ann Brunskill, a modern artist and private printer. The work contains her eight etchings illustrating the four fables and was published in an edition of only fifty copies, of which the Library has number 20. Aesop was a popular author *par excellence* and has been published in a multitude of versions; this

particular one is very much a one-person production. As well as selecting the fables and making the etchings, Ann Brunskill set and printed the text on a hand press, dyed the cloth for the binding, and published the book through her own press, the World's End Press. Even such a small edition is aimed at the public, and its presence in the Library's Rare Books collection ensures both its preservation and its accessibility.

Facsimiles, or exact reproductions of an original, make rare works available to a new or expanded audience at a cost well below the price an original would command. If they are published in a limited edition they are rare in themselves and often, because of the effort which goes into their production, a limited edition is appropriate. A good example of this is a facsimile produced in 1976 by the Basilisk Press in London of *The Red Books of Humphry Repton*. Repton was an English landscape gardener whose work was at first influenced by Lancelot 'Capability' Brown, but who later moved to a style which was more natural, although still artistic. He worked for the most important noble families of his time, including the Prince Regent, and he published a number of books including *Observations on the Theory and Practice of Landscape Gardening*. His 'Red Books', however, were not published: they were a set of notebooks containing handwritten proposals for landscape works, with 'before and after' watercolour sketches—the 'after' being revealed by lifting a flap over part of the original picture. The technical difficulties in the making of the facsimile were considerable, particularly in ensuring consistent colour reproduction for each complete image and its overlay, particularly as some had more than one overlay. The three facsimile *Red Books* are accompanied by a book by Edward Malins, which discusses Repton's career and influence, and the set was issued in a large box with a compartment for each volume.

A 'true' miniature book is one measuring 75 mm (about 3") or less in height, but for practical reasons many libraries treat all books up to a height of 100 mm (about 4") as miniatures: very small books need special storage as they are so easily lost or damaged in a conventional stack. Fitting well into the 'true miniature' group are the books produced in Worcester, Massachusetts by Achille J. St Onge, who published a miniature each year for almost fifty years. The Library has several of his tiny books, including *The Eulogy to United States Senator Robert F. Kennedy by His Brother, United States Senator Edward M. Kennedy, Delivered at St Patrick's Cathedral, New York City, June 8th, 1968*. The work is bound in dark green morocco with gold tooling, and has a photograph of RFK tipped in as a frontispiece. Because the interest in this particular subject was so great, the size of the edition was much larger than is usual for miniature books—2000 copies were printed.

It is easy to assume that, because rare books are stored and used under secure conditions, they are neither accessible nor relevant today. The security which libraries provide for such material is simply for its protection, and to ensure that these books continue to be available for users both now and in the future. The National Library has always had a policy of making its Rare Books collection as freely available as is consistent with its preservation, and use of the collection is increasing significantly. The books were, after all, produced in the first place for people to read, and they continue to be read, both for themselves and as primary source material. In belonging now to the National Library of Australia, these treasures also belong to the people of Australia.

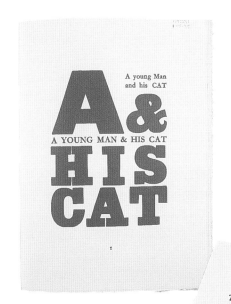

'A Young Man & His Cat': the chapter opening from *Four Fables*, presented by Ann Brunskill and World's End Press in an edition of 50 copies, each with five artist's proofs.

The colophon from *Four Fables*, giving details of this fine limited edition.

73

Chapter notes and sources

Full details of the principal items or collections described in each chapter are given below. Where appropriate, collection identifiers are enclosed in parentheses at the end of each entry.

Introduction

1 The People's Treasures: A Celebration of Collectors and Collections in the National Library of Australia, National Library Gallery, 9 June–5 September 1993, curated by Michael Richards.

2 *Treasures of the British Library.* Compiled by Nicolas Barker. London: The British Library, 1988. p. 11.

———

Spiller, John. [Marble Plaque of John Webber]. c.1790. (NK 1110)

Gill, S.T. *Country NW of Tableland, Aug. 22.* Watercolour, [c.1846].

Corsali, Andrea. *Lettera di Andrea Corsali allo Illustrissimo Signore Duca Juliano de Medici.* [Florence, between 1516 and 1523]. (MS 7860)

People's treasures, people's history

1 Osborn, Andrew and Margaret. *The Commonwealth Parliamentary Library, 1901–27 and the Origins of the National Library of Australia.* Canberra: Department of the Parliamentary Library in association with the National Library of Australia, 1989. pp. 18, 45.

2 Quoted in ibid., p. 12. Cf. Biskup, Peter. *Library Models and Library Myths: the Early Years of the National Library of Australia.* Historical Bibliography Monographs, no. 11. Kensington, NSW: History Project Incorporated, [1983].

3 Quoted in Osborn, p. 125.

4 Thompson, John. 'The Nan Kivell legacy' in Marian Minson, *Encounter with Eden: New Zealand 1770–1870.* Wellington, NZ: National Library of New Zealand, 1990. pp. 7–11.

5 Osborn, p. 130.

6 Powell, Graeme and Adrian Cunningham, 'Historical sources and the tyranny of distance: the achievements of the Australian Joint Copying Project' in *Australian Studies: Acquisition and Collection Development for Libraries.* Edited by G.E. Gorman. London: Mansell, 1992. pp. 251–62.

7 Mitchell, Ann M. 'Doctor Frederick Watson and *Historical Records of Australia', Historical Studies* vol. 20, no. 79, October 1982. pp. 171–97.

8 Osborn, pp. 100–1.

9 *The Hazel de Berg Recordings: from the Oral History Collection of the National Library of Australia.* Canberra: National Library of Australia, 1989.

10 Powell, G.T. 'Modes of acquisition: the growth of the Manuscript collection of the National Library of Australia', in *Library for the Nation.* Edited by Peter Biskup and Margaret Henty. Canberra: Australian Academic & Research Libraries with the National Library of Australia, 1991. pp. 74–5.

———

Wilson, Hardy. *George's Hall, George's River, N.S.W.* Pencil drawing, 1916.

Bardin, W. & J.M. [*Terrestial Globe*]. 1814.

The heart of the matter

1 *Guide to the Collections.* Compiled by C.A. Burmester. Canberra: National Library of Australia, 1974. Vol. 1, p. 467.

———

Queiros, Pedro Fernades de. *Terra Australis Incognita, or, A New Southern Discovery.* 2nd edn. London: Printed for William Bray, [1723?]. (Pethpam 2789)

Dampier, William. *A New Voyage Round the World ...* 2nd edn. London, 1697. (NK 1509)

Pelsaert, Francisco. *Ongeluckige Voyagie, van't Schip* Batavia, *nae de Oost-Indien ...* Amsterdam: Voor Jan Jansz, 1647. (994 PEL)

Hawkesworth, J. *An Account of the Voyages Undertaken by the Order of His Present Majesty for Making Discoveries in the Southern Hemisphere, and Successively Performed by Commodore Byron, Captain Wallis, Captain Carteret and Captain Cook, in the* Dolphin, *the* Swallow *and the* Endeavour. *Drawn up from the journals which were kept by the several Commanders, and from the papers of J. Banks.* 3 vols. London: W. Strahan & T. Cadell, 1773. (NK 5634)

Cook, James, Captain. *A Voyage Towards the South Pole and Round the World, Performed in His Majesty's Ships the* Resolution *and* Adventure, *in the Years 1772, 1773, 1774 and 1775.* 2 vols. London: W. Strahan & T. Cadell, 1777. (NK 5677)

Cook, James, Captain. *A Voyage to the Pacific Ocean, Undertaken by the Command of His Majesty, for Making Discoveries in the Northern Hemisphere ... Performed Under the Direction of Captains Cook, Clerke and Gore, in His Majesty's Ships, the* Resolution *and* Discovery, *in the Years 1776, 1777, 1778, 1779 and 1780.* 3 vols. London: Printed by W. & A. Strahan for G. Nicol & T. Cadell, 1784. (NK 1428)

Magra, James. *A Journal of a Voyage Round the World, in His Majesty's Ship* Endeavour, *in the Years 1768, 1769, 1770, and 1771.* London: Becket & de Hondt, 1771. (NK 5081)

Samwell, David. *A Narrative of the Death of Captain James Cook ...* London: Printed for G.G.J. & J. Robinson, 1786. (NK 35/NK 4421/RBN 920 COO)

A Catalogue of the Different Specimens of Cloth Collected in the Three Voyages of Captain Cook ... London: Printed for Alexander Shaw, 1787. (F 7143)

Dalrymple, Alexander. *A Serious Admonition to the Publick, on the Intended Thief-Colony at Botany Bay.* London: Printed by George Bigg, for John Sewell, 1786. (F 6)

R—, G—. *Proposals, for Employing Convicts, Within this Kingdom ...* London, 1787. (F 26)

White, John. *Journal of a Voyage to New South Wales ...* London: Printed for J. Debrett, 1790. (F 97)

Phillip, Arthur. *The Voyage of Governor Phillip to Botany Bay ...* London: Printed for John Stockdale, 1789. (F 47)

Officer, An. *An Authentic Journal of the Expedition Under Commodore Phillips to Botany Bay ...* London: Printed for C. Forster, 1789. (F 45)

Tench, Watkin. *A Narrative of the Expedition to Botany-Bay; with an Account of New South Wales, its Productions, Inhabitants, &c. ...* London: Printed for J. Debrett; New York: Reprinted by T. & J. Swords, 1789. (F 48a)

Flinders, Matthew. *Observations on the Coasts of Van Diemen's Land, on Bass's Strait and Its Islands, and on Part of the Coasts of New South Wales ...* London: Printed by John Nichols, 1801. (F 329)

Blaxland, Gregory. *A Journal of a Tour of Discovery Across the Blue Mountains in New South Wales.* London: B.J. Holdsworth, 1823. (F 894)

Hume, Hamilton. *A Brief Statement of Facts in Connexion with an Overland Expedition from Lake George to Port Phillip, in 1824.* Sydney: J. Moore, 1855. (F 10662)

Giles, Ernest. *The Journal of a Forgotten Expedition.* Reprinted from the 'Adelaide Observer'. Adelaide: W.K. Thomas & Co., 1880. (F 9913)

Collins, David. *An Account of the English Colony in New South Wales with Remarks on the Dispositions, Customs, Manners, &c. of the Native Inhabitants of that Country ...* London: Printed for T. Cadell, Jun. & W. Davies, 1798. (F 263)

Clark, John Heaviside. *Field Sports, &c. &c. of the Native Inhabitants of New South Wales ...* London: Edward Orme, 1813. (F 551)

Clark, John Heaviside. *Smoking Out the Opposum.* Handcoloured aquatint, 1813. Plate from Clark's *Field Sports, &c. &c...* (NK 628/1)

Threlkeld, Rev. Lancelot Edward. *Specimens of a Dialect, of the Aborigines of New South Wales ...* Sydney: Printed at the 'Monitor Office', by Arthur Hill, 1827. (F 1147)

Threlkeld, Rev. Lancelot Edward. *A Statement Chiefly Relating to the Formation and Abandonment of a Mission to the Aborigines of New South Wales.* Sydney: Printed by R. Howe, Government Printer, 1828. (F 1219)

Slater, John. *A Description of Sydney, Parramatta, Newcastle, &c. Settlements in New South Wales, with Some Account of the Manners and Employment of the Convicts ...* Nottingham: Sutton & Son, 1819. (F 768)

Wells, Thomas E. *Michael Howe, the Last and Worst of the Bush Rangers of Van Diemen's Land. Narrative of the Chief Atrocities Committed by this Great Murderer and His Associates, During a Period of Six Years in Van Diemen's Land*. Hobart Town: Printed by Andrew Bent, 1818. (F 716)

Wentworth, William Charles. *A Statistical, Historical, and Political Description of the Colony of New South Wales, and its Dependent Settlements in Van Diemen's Land ...* London: Printed for G. & B. Whittaker, 1819. (F 771)

Evans, George William. *A Geographical, Historical and Topographical Description of Van Diemen's Land, with Important Hints to Emigrants ...* London: Printed for John Souter, 1822. (F 861)

Curr, Edward. *An Account of the Colony of Van Diemen's Land ...* London: Printed for George Cowie & Co., 1824. (F 938)

Atkinson, James. *An Account of the State of Agriculture & Grazing in New South Wales ...* London: J. Cross, 1826. (F 1054)

Lewin, John William. *Birds of New Holland, with Their Natural History. Collected, Engraved, and Faithfully Painted after Nature*. London: J. White & S. Bagster, 1808. (F 465)

Lewin, John William. *Birds of New South Wales with Their Natural History*. Sydney: Printed by G. Howe, 1813. (F 557)

Smith, Sir James Edward. *A Specimen of the Botany of New Holland*. London: J. Sowerby, 1793. (F 170)

Shaw, George. *Zoology of New Holland*. London: J. Sowerby, 1794. (F 196)

West, Absalom. *Views of New South Wales*. 12 plates. Sydney, 1813. (F 570a)

Earle, Augustus. *Views in Australia*. Sydney, c.1826. (F 1070)

Earle, Augustus. *Sydney, H.M. Ship Warspite 74 Guns*. Handcoloured lithograph, [c.1825]. Plate no. 4 in Earle's *Views in Australia*.

Field, Barron. *First Fruits of Australian Poetry*. Sydney, 1819; 2nd edn. Sydney, 1823. (F 738/F 906)

Wentworth, William Charles. *Australasia*. London: G. & W.B. Whittaker, 1823. (F 924)

Tompson, Charles. *Wild Notes, from the Lyre of a Native Minstrel*. Sydney: Printed by Robert Howe, Government Printer, 1826. (F 1093)

Savery, Henry. *Quintus Servinton. A Tale, Founded upon Incidents of Real Occurrence*. Hobart Town: Henry Melville, Printer, 1830; London: Smith, Elder & Co., 1832. (F 1589)

Barton, Charlotte. *A Mother's Offering to Her Children*: By a Lady. Sydney: Printed at the 'Gazette' Office, 1841. (F 3158)

Renneville, Madame de. *Les Enfans de 15 Ans: Histoires à mes Jeunes Amis*. Limoges [France]: Barbou, [c.1814]. (N 843.7 R415en)

Fouinet, E. *Allan: le Jeune Déporté à Botany-Bay*. Paris: Désirée Eymery à la Bibliothèque d'Éducation, 1836. (F 2123b)

Returned Digger, A. *Six Years in Australia: Its Present Condition and Future Prospects. Descriptive, Entertaining and Instructive*. Manchester: James Cheetham, 1857. (F 14882)

Sources for Australian studies

1 *With Captain James Cook in the Antarctic and Pacific: The Private Journal of James Burney. Second Lieutenant of the Adventure on Cook's Second Voyage 1772–1773*. Edited and with an introduction by Beverley Hooper. Canberra: National Library of Australia, 1975.

2 *The Bligh Notebook: 'Rough Account— Lieutenant Wm Bligh's Voyage in the Bounty's Launch from the Ship to Tofua & from Thence to Timor' 28 April to 14 June 1789*. Transcription and facsimile edited by John Bach. Canberra: National Library of Australia, 1986.

3 *Dark and Hurrying Days: Menzies' 1941 Diary*. Edited by A.W. Martin and Patsy Hardy. Canberra: National Library of Australia, 1993.

4 *Letters of Vance and Nettie Palmer 1915–1963*. Selected and edited by Vivian Smith. Canberra: National Library of Australia, 1977.

————

Australasian Federation League of New South Wales. Records. (MS 47)

Banks, Sir Joseph. Papers. (MS 9)

Burney, James. Journal, 1772–73. (MS 3244)

Cook, James, Captain. Journal of HMS *Endeavour*, 1768–71. (MS 1)

Gore, John. Journal of HMS *Dolphin*, 1766–68. (MS 4)

Bowes Smyth, Arthur. Journal, 1787–89. (MS 4568)

King, Philip Gidley. Journal, 1791–96.
(MS 70)

King Family. Annotated copy of John
Hunter's *An Historical Journal of the
Transactions at Port Jackson and Norfolk
Island*, 1793. (MS 8572)

Bligh, William. Notebook, 1789.
(MS 5393)

Brisbane, Sir Thomas. Papers.
(MS 4036)

Lang, John Dunmore. Papers.
(MS 3267)

Fawkner, John Pascoe. Journal, 1835–36.
(MS 3224)

Franklin, Jane, Lady. Papers. (MS 114)

Norcock, John. Journal, 1835–37.
(MS 5896)

Weynton, Alexander. Journals, 1847–60.
(MS 7130)

Barton, Sir Edmund. Papers. (MS 51)

Groom, Sir Littleton E. Papers.
(MS 236)

Deakin, Alfred. Papers. (MS 1540)

Hughes, William M. Papers. (MS 1538)

Eggleston, Sir Frederic. Papers.
(MS 423)

Latham, Sir John. Papers. (MS 1009)

Menzies, Sir Robert G. Papers.
(MS 4936)

Tennyson, Hallam, 2nd Baron, and Lady
Tennyson. Papers. (MS 479)

Novar, Sir Ronald C. Munro-Ferguson,
1st Viscount. Papers. (MS 696)

Trollope, Anthony. Manuscript of
Australia. (MS 187)

Richardson, Henry Handel. Papers.
(MS 133)

Slessor, Kenneth. Papers. (MS 3020)

Williamson, David. Papers. (MS 7378)

Stead, Christina. Papers. (MS 4967)

Prichard, Katharine Susannah. Papers.
(MS 6201)

White, Patrick. Manuscript of *Memoirs of
Many in One*. (MS 8293)

Palmer, Vance and Nettie. Papers.
(MS 1174)

Antill, John. Papers. (MS 437)

Helpmann, Sir Robert. Papers.
(MS 7161)

Friend, Donald. Papers. (MS 5959)

Bates, Daisy M. Papers. (MS 365)

Monash, Sir John. Papers. (MS 1884)

Bradman, Sir Donald. Albums of
cuttings and photographs. (MS 7035)

Australian Inland Mission. Records.
(MS 5574)

———

Australia's cultural heritage

[Arthur Bate, Rose Boxsell, Mildred Bate
and Nellie Boxsell, taken at Boxsell
House]. Photograph, c.1895. (Tilba
Tilba collection)

Roberts, Tom. *Bourke Street, Melbourne*.
Also known as *Allegro con Brio, Bourke Street
West*. Oil on canvas lined on
composition board, [c.1886].

Gill, S.T. *Gt. Bourke St. Looking East from
Queen St., Melbourne*. Print, 1857.
Engraved by J. Tingle. Plate 46 in
Victoria Illustrated. Melbourne: Sands &
Kenny, 1857.

Crépin, Louis-Philippe. *Inauguration du
Monument Élevé par l'Astrolabe à La Pérouse
à Vanikoro, 14th March, 1828*. Oil on
canvas. [1831?]. Attributed to de
Sainson by Rex Nan Kivell.
(NK 11641)

Hunter, John. *Birds and Flowers of New
South Wales Drawn on the Spot in 1788, '89 &
'90*. 1 sketchbook (100 watercolours),
1788–90. (NK 2039)

Martens, Conrad. *Sydney from the North
Shore*. Watercolour, [184–]. (NK 181)

Earle, Augustus. *View from the Summit of
Mount York, Looking Towards Bathurst Plains,
Convicts Breaking Stones, N.S. Wales*.
Watercolour, c.1826. (NK 12/23)

Earle, Augustus. *Bungaree, a Native Chief of
New South Wales*. Handcoloured
lithograph, 1830. (NK 2652)

Counihan, Noel. *Portrait of Vance Palmer*.
Oil on composition board, 1953.
(R 3881)

Cazneaux, Harold. *Knock-off Time,
Newcastle*. Photograph, [193–]. (C 14/2)

Hurley, Frank. *The* Endurance *with an
Iceberg Bearing upon It. Shackleton Expedition*.
Glass negative, [1914–16].

Prout, John Skinner. *Broulee, N.S.W.*
Watercolour, [1843]. (NK 311/7)

Vasilieff, Danila. *Portrait of Basil Burdett*.
Oil on wood panel, [c.1930].

Perry, Adelaide. *Portrait of Dame Mary
Gilmore*. Oil on plywood panel on
composition board, 1928.

Rare maps in context

1   Harley, J.B. 'Silences and secrecy: the hidden agenda of cartography in early modern Europe', *Imago Mundi* vol. 40, 1988, pp. 57–76.

2   Richardson, W.A.R. *The Portuguese Discovery of Australia: Fact or Fiction?* Canberra: National Library of Australia, 1989.

3   Williamson, Ian P. 'The development of the cadastral survey system in New South Wales', *Australian Surveyor* vol. 32, no. 1, 1984, pp. 2–20.

———

Ortelius, Abraham. *Maris Pacifici (quod vulgo Mar del Zur) cum Regionibus Circumiacentibus, Insalisque in Codem Passim Sparsis, Novissima Descriptio.* [Antverpiae: C. Plantin], 1589. Published in *Theatrum Orbis Terrarum.* [Antwerp: C. Plantin, 1592]. (RM 164)

Ortelius, Abraham. *Indiae Orientalis Insularum que Adiacentium Typus.* [1570]. (T 937)

De Jode, Cornelis. *Novae Guineae Forma, & Situs.* Published in De Jode's Speculum Orbis Terrae. 2nd edn. Antwerp, 1593. (T 385)

Vallard, Nicholas. *The First Map of Australia.* [Chester, (Cheshire): McGahey, 1856. Originally published in Vallard's *Sea Atlas*, 1547. (RM 1819)

Hondius, Henricus. *India quae Orientalis Dicitur, et Insulae Adiacentes.* [Amsterdam, 1633]. (T 721)

Doncker, Hendrick. *De Zee-Atlas Ofte Water-Waerald* [The Sea Atlas of the Water World]. Amsterdam: Hendrick Doncker, 1659. (RA10) (Reproduced on microfiche, Canberra: National Library of Australia, 1987.)

Doncker, Hendrick. *Oosterdeel van Oost Indien Streckende van Cilon tot Japan en tot de Landrones Ilanden.* Amsterdam: Hendrick Doncker, [1696]. (T 452)

Dudley, Sir Robert. *Arcano del Mare.* 2nd edn. Florence: Giuseppe Cocchini, 1661. (RA 248)

Sanson, Nicolas. *Mappe-monde: ou Carte Generale du Monde Dessignée en Deux Plan-Hemispheres.* Paris, [1651]. (NK 1561)

Robert de Vaugondy, G. & D. *Carte Reduite de l'Australasie pour Servir a la Lecture de l'Histoire des Terres Australes.* [Paris]: G. Delahaye, 1756. (T 1002)

Coronelli, Vincenzo. [*Northern Australia*]. [Venice, 1696]. (T 352)

Coronelli, Vincenzo. [*Terrestial Globe*]. Venice, c.1690. Facsimile, J.C. Eade, 1978.

Coronelli, Vincenzo. [*Celestial Globe*]. Venice, 1700. Facsimile, J.C. Eade, 1978.

Buache, Philippe. *Carte Physique de la Grande Mer ci-devant Nommée Mer du Sud ou Pacifique ...* 1754. (T 272)

Whitchurch, W. *Chart of Part of the South Sea Shewing the Tracts and Discoveries Made His Majesty's Ships* Dolphin Commodore Byron & Tamar *Capn Mouat 1765* Dolphin *Capn Wallis, &* Swallow, *Capn Carteret 1767* and Endeavour, *Lieutenant Cooke 1769.* London, 1773. (T 321)

Bowen, Emanuel. *A Complete Map of the Southern Continent Survey'd by Capt. Abel Tasman & Depicted by Order of the East India Company in Holland in the Stadt House at Amsterdam.* Issued in John Harris' *Navigantium atque Itinerantium Bibliotheca, or, a Complete Collection of Voyages and Travels.* London, 1744. (T 241)

Birmingham, Frederick William. *Map of the Town of Portland in the Colony of Victoria.* [Victoria]: F.W. Birmingham, 1853. (F 874)

A New Plan of the Settlements in New South Wales, taken by order of government, July 20th 1810. Sydney: William Dymock, 1810. (F 377)

Grey, George. *Supposed Native Tombs Discovered on the N.W. Coast of New Holland, 7th April 1838.* (NK 1315A)

A New Map of the Province of Auckland. London: Edward Stanford, 1865. (RM 491)

Chapman's Map of the North Island of New Zealand Including the Provinces of Auckland, Taranaki, Hawke's Bay and Wellington, with all the Recent Surveys. Auckland: Geo. T. Chapman, [1866]. (RM 494)

Society for Promoting Christian Knowledge. *New Zealand.* London: Stanford's Geographical Establishment, 1874. (RM 498)

The Gold Regions of Australia. And the Road to the Diggings. London: *Lloyd's Weekly*, [n.d.] (RM 759)

Wyld, James. *Map of the Gold Regions of Australia.* London: Wyld, 1851. (RM 773)

Arrowsmith, John. *The South Eastern Portion of Australia*. Compiled from the colonial surveys, and from details furnished by exploratory expeditions. London: John Arrowsmith, 1852. (T 98)

Johnston, W. & A.K. *Colony of New South Wales and Victoria*. [1852]. (T 763)

Betts Map of the Gold Regions of Australia. London: John Betts, [1855]. (NK 2456/111)

Ham, Thomas. *Ham's Map of the Routes to the Mt Alexander & Ballarat Gold Diggings*. Melbourne: Ham, 1852. (RM 960)

The Digger's Road Guide to the Gold Mines of Victoria and the Country Extending 210 Miles Round Melbourne ... Melbourne: S.T. Leigh, 1853. (RM 956, NK 2456/133)

The Emigrants' Guide Map to the Port Curtis Gold Fields and Part of North Eastern Australia. Melbourne: Edward Gilks, 1858. (F 494)

Road Map and Guide to the Gold Fields with the Newest Tracks to the Snowy River. Compiled from the most authenticated government maps. Victoria and New South Wales. Melbourne: Fergusson & Mitchell, [1860]. (RM 907)

Sketch Map of New South Wales Showing the Localities of the Principal Minerals 1876. Sydney: Thomas Richards Government Printer, 1876. (T 1244)

Taylor, Norman. *Learmonth*. Melbourne: James Finnie, 1882. (RM 2987)

Cooper, W.M. *Tourist Map of the Blue Mountains, New South Wales*. Sydney: Government Printing Office, 1885. (RM 1826)

Slight, James. *Victoria Classified According to its Productiveness*. [Melbourne?]: Commissioner of Crown Lands and Survey, 1901. (RM 2087)

Beaumont, Sidney & D.H. Souter, *Aeroplane View of Sydney 1914 ...* Sydney: H.E.C. Robinson, 1914. (F 896)

The Inlander. Sydney: Samuel & Lees, 1922. (MS 6234)

Vernon, W.L. *Map of District North of the Hunter River*. Specially prepared for the April field manoeuvres, 1907. Sydney: W.A. Gullick, 1907. (F 909)

Orographical Map of the Dardanelles. Reproduced from captured Turkish maps. Egypt: Survey Dept, 1915. (F 238)

Davies, E.T.L. [*Plane Table Survey of Anglesea, Victoria*], sheet 5. [n.d.]

Mager, John F. *Lutheran Mission Madang in Territory of New Guinea*. Saint Paul, Minn: American Lutheran Church, 1936. (F 904)

A journey to Asia

[*The Tale of Genji*]. 28 vols. [Japan, n.d.]

[*Khmer Tripitaka*]. Phnom Penh: Cambodian Royal National Library, 1931–. (Khmer collection)

[*Life of the Minorities in Southwest China*]. 2 vols. [China, 18–?]

Tibetan Buddhist Canon. USA: Dharma Press, 1981.

Koryo Taejang-gyong [Tripitaka Koreana]. 1340 vols. Reprinted Pan Korea Book Co., 1964–68. (OK 1803)

Kan Song Phanuat Nai Ratchakan Thi 7 [Thai cremation volume]. Bangkok: Wat Bowon niwet wihan, 1985.

Samgang Haengsilto [The Three Principles of Basic Human Relationships]. [1490]. (McLaren–Human collection)

Taiping Rebellion wall poster. China, 1853.

Rare books

Bible. Latin. Vulgate. [Single leaf from Leviticus, chs VI & VII. Mainz: Johann Gutenberg, c.1455.] (RBRS 12)

Biblia Latina. 2 vols. Paterson, NJ: Pageant Books, 1961. Facsimile of the Gutenberg Bible, also known as the 42-line Bible or Biblia sacra. (RBf 093 BIB)

de Voragine, Jacobus. *Legenda aurea*. Venice: Christophorus Arnoldus, [before 6 May] 1478. (RBRS de Vesci 856)

Schedel, Hartmann. *Liber cronicarum*. Nuremberg: Anton Koberger, 12 July 1493. (RBRS 5)

Dürer, Albrecht. *Passio christi ab Alberto Dürer*. Nuremberg: Albrecht Dürer, 1511. (RBRS 13)

Higden, Ranulf. [Single leaf from *Polychronicon*. Westminster: William Caxton, after 2 July 1482.] Leaf detached from Isaac, book 2, chapter 11. (RBRS 8)

de Voragine, Jacobus. *The Legende Named in Latyn* Legenda aurea *that is to Saye in Englysshe the Golden Legende ...* London: Wynkyn de Worde, 1527. (RB CLI 3253)

Shakespeare, William. *The Merchant of Venice*. London: Isaac Iaggard & Ed. Blount, 1623. Detached from his *Comedies, Histories and Tragedies*. (RBRS 11)

Locke, John. *An Essay Concerning Humane Understanding*. 4th edn. with large additions. London: for Awnsham & John Churchill & Samuel Manship, 1700. (RBq MISC 2068)

Johnson, Samuel. *A Dictionary of the English Language: in which the Words are Deduced from Their Originals, and Illustrated in Their Different Significations by Examples from the Best Writers*. 2 vols. London: by W. Strahan, for J. & P. Knapton; T. & T. Longman; C. Hitch & L. Howes; A. Millar; and R. & J. Dodsley, 1755. First edition. (RBq MISC 33)

Smith, Adam. *An Inquiry into the Nature and Causes of the Wealth of Nations*. 2 vols. London: for W. Strahan & T. Cadell, 1776. First edition. (RB Ec 6594)

Procès-verbaux de l'Assemblée Nationale, Contenant Les Articles qu'elle a Adoptés de la Déclaration des Droits de l'Homme & du Citoyen ... Paris: Au Bureau du Journal Général de la Cour & de la Ville, 1789. (RB 944.04 REV box 9, AN 1691)

Malthus, Thomas Robert. *Principles of Political Economy Considered with a View to Their Practical Application*. London: Murray, 1820. Presentation copy of the first edition from the author to Lord Grenville. (RBRS Ec 4235)

Owen, Robert. *A New View of Society, or, Essays on the Principle of the Formation of Human Character and the Application of the Principle to Practice*. London: for Cadell & Davies, 1813–14. First edition. (RB Ec 5006)

Buffon, Georges Louis Leclerc, comte de. *Buffon's Natural History ...* 10 vols. with notes by the translator [J.S. Barr]. London: for the Proprietor and sold by H.D. Symonds, 1797–1807. (RB 570 BUF)

The Order of Chivalry. [Translated from the French by William Caxton, edited by F.S. Ellis] [with] *L'Ordene de Chevalerie* [with translation by William Morris]. [London: Kelmscott Press, 1892–93.] (RB 094 ORD)

Ramsaye, Terry. *A Million and One Nights; a History of the Motion Picture*. 2 vols. New York: Simon & Schuster, 1926. Number 98 of an edition of 327 copies signed by Thomas A. Edison and the author. (RB MOD 23)

Matrix: a Review for Printers and Bibliophiles. Andoversford, Glos: Whittington Press, 1981–. (RB 686.205 MAT)

Aesop. *Four Fables*. [Illustrated by] Ann Brunskill. London: World's End Press, 1972. Edition limited to fifty copies. (RBf 096.1 A254)

Repton, Humphry. *The Red Books of Humphry Repton*. 4 vols. London: The Basilisk Press, 1976. Number 240 of an edition limited to 515 copies. (RBef 712.0922 R426)

Kennedy, Edward M. *The Eulogy to United States Senator Robert F. Kennedy by His Brother, United States Senator Edward M. Kennedy, Delivered at St Patrick's Cathedral, New York City, June 8th, 1968*. Worcester, Mass: Achille J. St Onge, [1968]. Edition limited to 2000 copies. (RB min 973.920924

THE CONTRIBUTORS

John Thompson is Director, Australian Collection Promotion in the National Library of Australia. He began his career in the State Library of Victoria and in 1979 joined the National Library where he has worked since in a number of positions including that of Director, Australian Collections and Services. He has taken a keen interest in the development of the Library's collections and has written extensively about its special role as custodian of Australia's documentary heritage.

Stuart Macintyre is the Ernest Scott Professor of History at the University of Melbourne and a member of the National Library of Australia Council. He is the author of *The Succeeding Age 1901–1942*, volume 4 of *The Oxford History of Australia*, and *A Colonial Liberalism: The Lost World of Three Victorian Visionaries*, where he explored the liberal tradition from which the Australian statesman Alfred Deakin emerged.

Jonathan Wantrup is one of Australia's leading antiquarian book experts, well recognised both in Australia and overseas. His authoritative *Australian Rare Books 1788–1900* is generally recognised as the standard work on the subject; he has also written several other publications dealing with early Australian books. Between 1989 and 1990 Jonathan Wantrup was Director of Sotheby's Australia book department. In 1991 he joined Anne McCormick and Derek McDonnell as a director of Hordern House Rare Books, the internationally respected firm of antiquarian booksellers in Sydney.

Graeme Powell joined the National Library of Australia in 1967. He became Manuscript Librarian in 1969 and has been involved in collecting manuscripts ever since. In 1978 he went to London to be the Australian Joint Copying Project officer, eventually returning to Australia to his old position as Manuscript Librarian in 1987.

Sasha Grishin studied art history at the universities of Melbourne, Moscow, London and Oxford and has served several terms as visiting scholar at Harvard University. He has published extensively in contemporary and medieval art and is presently completing a three volume publication titled *S.T. Gill and his Audiences*. Since 1977 he has been the art critic for *The Canberra Times*, the year in which he founded the Fine Art Programme at the Australian National University, which later became the Department of Art History in which he now teaches.

Terry Birtles is Associate Professor in Applied Geography at the University of Canberra. He has published extensively on social and economic geography, the urban history of Canberra, and regional development in eastern Australia. He is a member of the Australian Institute of Cartographers and has served on the Institute's editorial board for twenty-two years.

Andrew Gosling is Chief Librarian, Asia in the Asian Collections Section of the National Library of Australia. He completed a Master of Arts (Asian Studies) degree at the Australian National University and joined the National Library in 1973. From 1979 to 1983 he was attached to the Australian Embassy in Jakarta as the Library's Indonesian Acquisition Officer.

Margaret Dent is a senior librarian in the National Library's Information Services Branch. Her background is varied and includes language studies for her first degree and work in a range of libraries such as the University of Sydney, the Royal Borough of Kensington and Chelsea Library, Australian Bureau of Statistics libraries in Sydney and Canberra, and the Australian Reference Section of the National Library. She has had a long involvement working with the National Library's rare book collection and has developed an appreciative understanding of its strengths.